THE WRITTEN WORD

Also by Stephen White

Students, Scholars and Parents
Should We Now Believe the Warren Report?

The Written Word

AND ASSOCIATED DIGRESSIONS CONCERNED WITH THE WRITER AS CRAFTSMAN

by Stephen White

 A Cornelia & Michael Bessie Book

HARPER & ROW, PUBLISHERS, New York
Cambridge, Philadelphia, San Francisco, London
Mexico City, São Paulo, Sydney

Miriam
would have read this,
and purged it of its extravagances,
and liked it.

Permissions acknowledgments appear on page 225.

FIRST EDITION

Designer: Sidney Feinberg

This book was set in 10-point ComCom Gael by The Haddon Craftsmen, Inc.,
ComCom Division, Allentown, Pennsylvania, and printed and bound by The
Haddon Craftsmen, Inc., Scranton, Pennsylvania.

Library of Congress Cataloging in Publication Data
White, Stephen, 1915–
    The written word, and associated digressions concerned with the writer as
craftsman.
    "A Cornelia and Michael Bessie book."
    Includes index.
    1. English language—Rhetoric. I. Title.
PE1408.W5805 1984   808′.042   83–49058
ISBN 0–06–039035–2

---

84 85 86 87 88 10 9 8 7 6 5 4 3 2 1

Contents

                                    And every phrase
And sentence that is right (where every word is at home,
Taking its place to support the others,
The word neither diffident nor ostentatious,
The easy commerce of the old and the new,
The common word exact without vulgarity,
The formal word precise but not pedantic,
The complete consort dancing together)
Every phrase and every sentence is an end and a beginning,
Every poem an epitaph.

    T. S. ELIOT, "Little Gidding"

The state of American society not being all I could ask, I suppose I am obliged at the outset to warn that you are no more likely to see "he or she" or "him or her" in these pages than you are likely to see "goose or gander" on a restaurant menu, and for exactly the same reason: In the English language such words as "men" and "he" are in the same category as "duck" and "goose" and "governor." They are unsigned, and within the appropriate context carry no denotation of sex. In some instances, a word such as "male" must be used or in some circles the word "men" employed as an adjective: "I had a man teacher in physics." "Women," on the other hand, always means "women." This appears to me sexism at its worst, obliging men to share their word whereas women have "women" all to themselves. But I am not one to grumble. Language evolves, and it may be that one day all such words will be signed. It makes for ugly speech patterns and ugly writing patterns, but no matter, I suppose.

Introduction

Some years ago, being thirteen or fourteen years old at the time, I was asked, or offered, a favor by a high-school classmate with modest dreams of glory. He proposed to become big man on campus, although it was a big-city high school and had no campus. As a stage of his road to glory, he wished to become editor of the school's literary magazine, which had quite a reputation among schools lacking any noticeable football team. He was not to be deterred by his inability to write coherent English prose or poesy. He suggested that I handle that part of the task; there would be a buck or two in it for me now and then.

All that was quite a while ago—Hoover was President at the time—and I have been writing for money, or inner satisfaction, or both, from that day to this. I may say modestly that I was an immediate success, for my classmate duly became editor. What happened to him thereafter I do not know. Later assignments were by no means uniformly triumphs, but one way or another I have made my way since then by my pen, although it was not always obvious that writing was what I was really doing. Writing intended for only one reader, or a few dozen, is still writing as I define it.

I have at one time or another written books, newspaper articles, magazine articles, plays, motion pictures, television programs, radio programs, short stories, essays, reviews, advertising, and handbills decrying the Nineteenth Amendment. I am sure I have left something out. I have never written a novel, although I tried once. My motion pictures were also not very good. I never made wealthy, but I never made destitute, either.

The newspaper articles that I wrote may be subdivided into garden-variety reporting, sports, drama criticism, editorials, science writing, national correspondence, foreign correspondence, city hall, the statehouse and the Capitol. The other tasks were equally various, or more so.

I enter these credentials not out of vainglory but out of necessity. I have set out to write a book about the written word and language in general, thereby entering territory well occupied by scholars. I am not a scholar, and have never intended to be one. I am a working stiff. Scholars are grammarians, or linguists, or lexicographers, or classicists, or members of departments given over to the study of literature. I am poaching. They will be quite justified when they sputter, "Why, the fellow hasn't even read *the literature!*" True enough. I have read a good deal of literature, but I have never read the literature, which is a different matter entirely, as any graduate student can tell you. I wish I had, but I have been busy.

I have written a great deal, and thought about writing a great deal. That is all the territory I claim. Whether I know anything at all of what I am writing about here we shall all find out.

Still, I cannot quite leave it at that. A literary critic back in good Queen Victoria's day once began his dissection of the volume before him as follows: "This gentleman has gone out of his way to write a book." Curmudgeon or not, he may have been on firm ground. There should be a reason.

There is. It is important that people continue to write, and that they write with some degree of skill. I am not thinking of those few we think of as writers: the Saul Bellows and the John Cheevers and the Rebecca Wests, if you will, or the Judith Krantzes or the Dick Francises. Neither am I ignoring those estimable folks. What I have in mind is everyone, or so nearly everyone as to make no difference.

Nor am I referring to writing for publication, which is a most infrequent consequence of the act of writing, and most fortunately so. Only the smallest fraction of what is written, day after day, is read by anyone but him who wrote it and perhaps a handful of others.

It is important that people write, and I shall try to say why. If they do write, it is important that they write with reasonable skill, and I shall try to say what that means because I believe I can be useful. Modest aims. In the end, they are pedagogic aims, and why not?

I make no claim that I am writing any kind of handbook, in which one can look up what one wants to do before doing it, or find explicit instructions for the proper handling of metonymy. I shall be attempting rather to describe a craft than to provide instructions for its exercise. In short, I am tackling half a problem. I do not believe a craft can be exercised unless it is understood, nor can it be understood without its exercise. But the two can be considered separately, and for the most part it is the first of the two that concerns me here.

I have chosen to write in a most casual style, personal and discursive, intended to win acceptance rather than command it. The pages are sprinkled with "I" and "you" and "we." Formal writing is a good deal easier, but I enjoy this more. Those who do not are directed to the collected works of Immanuel Kant. But if I seem overly light-minded about the way I say things, be assured that I do not intend to be light-minded about what I say.

One more word, and we shall get about our business. I am foolhardy beyond the bounds of ordinary common sense; I am writing about writing. Like any book ever committed to honest paper, this one will abound in solecisms, grammatical errors, lapses of auctorial taste, infelicities, howlers, errors of judgment— all the abominations that confound the writer as he is at his work, and a few others inserted after the manuscript has been delivered. This would be bad enough if I were writing about algebraic topology, but in a book about writing! I am delivering myself into the hands of mine enemy; I am self-destructing. No matter. It is all in a good cause.

Chapter One

To Begin With

> . . . the theory of description matters most.
> It is the theory of the word for those
>
> For whom the making of the word
>   is the making of the world,
> The buzzing world and lisping firmament,
>
> It is a world of words to the end of it.
>
>   WALLACE STEVENS, "Description Without Place"

THE written word is our subject, and a most complicated subject it is. It began complicated, some millennia back, and like anything that necessarily falls into the hands of those who teach the young, it has become encrusted with nonsense, such as grave statements about the vocative mode. (My biases are not long in coming to light.) Complications encrusted with nonsense are nothing to toy with, and if a little introductory material will help before we get to the heart of the matter, we need not be edgy about it. Consequently, let me begin with a few words about the why and the how of all this, before we begin to tangle directly with the what.

Some write for money, and are generally doomed to disappointment; some write for their own amusement and begin to ask themselves, halfway through, what could have led them to believe even for a moment that writing is an amusing occupation. I am writing about writing primarily because I believe that writing is an extremely important activity, and because I have serious fears

1

about what might happen if the habit of writing were to wither away, as it begins to seem it might.

Since the evolution and the diffusion of that complicated invention known as the alphabet, the act of writing has infused the act of taking thought. To put the matter a good deal more simply than it deserves, the act of writing converts a thought into an object that can be handled, shared, scrutinized, adjusted, and above all discarded. Writing is by no means the only way of objectifying a thought, but it is the cheapest, the least cluttered, the most flexible, and quite possibly the very best, although at this moment I shall not insist upon that last characteristic, leaving it for later consideration, when I am fully warmed up.

It is also under attack as it has not been for two thousand years or more. Technology has devised whole batteries of devices that either make it unnecessary to write, or occupy time and effort that were once devoted to writing and reading. Where we once scribbled notes we now make telephone calls; where we once read of an evening we now sit before a television set; where we once subscribed to the local newspaper we now switch on the car radio during the drive home.

That battery of assaults upon the written word, taken wholly on its own terms, is easily brushed aside as a matter of no great consequence. The scribbled notes that have disappeared were after all largely devoid of content and have merely been replaced by equally empty telephone calls; the novels and magazines of fiction once so widely read were not a bit less shoddy than the television programs that have taken their place; the news, whether in print as it used to be or over the air as it is, remains almost entirely trivial, or sensational, or both. But in such arguments the central point is likely to be lost. The reliance upon the technologies is such as to destroy, for almost all of us, the habit of writing and even the habit of reading. When the habit goes, the skill goes. The tool rusts, or at the very least lies uncomfortably in the hand. It is there that the danger is to be found, and not in the minor perturbation that comes about when people become used to watching <u>Three's Company</u> instead of reading <u>Girl of the Limberlost</u>.

Clearly, I am not to be convinced that this is a small matter, and much of what I shall be writing is intended to clarify the nature of the problem that a good deal of communications technology imposes upon society, if that is not too grand a claim. But the end I have in view—the distant end, at this point—is pedagogic. Even in the face of the technologies, I am inclined to believe that there are fashions in which the habit of writing may be in some degree preserved, and that the technologies themselves can in some degree be called upon to assist. I hasten to add that I offer no panacea, and that preserving the habit will not be easy either for those who direct the effort or for those who actually exert it. But that is not the point from which to set forth; we must consider first, and for a good long while, writing itself.

I write in part to engage the reader in a consideration of the language he speaks and writes and takes for granted. As Alfred North Whitehead once pointed out, it is by no means easy to undertake an analysis of the obvious, but quite frequently most instructive. Since I find the whole matter to be well worth pursuing, I can hardly be blamed if I expect the reader to enjoy participating in the pursuit. But I wish to persuade as well, and I shall have a good deal to say about how writing might be taught to those engaged in passage from nursery school to the ranks of the learned.

No one, however, will learn to write by reading this book. No one will learn to write by reading <u>any</u> book. He will learn to write, if he learns at all, by writing and then reading what he has written. Sorry about that.

I want to begin by distinguishing between two uses of the written word, although as usual in any real world the distinctions fade at the margins. The margins can be ignored for the moment, although sooner or later they must be dealt with.

There is, to begin with, the kind of writing that may be found on the first page of your morning newspaper, or in the instruction manual that was included with your electric can opener, or in the Journal of the American Medical Association, or in the collected works of Isaac Asimov. All these employ the written word to describe something or another: in the instances given, what are described are respectively the state of the world, a working kitchen instrument, medical research, and advances in science and technology.

Beyond description, there may also be criticism. Explicit criticism will not necessarily be found on the first page of the newspaper, but if one reads carefully it is likely to be there one way or another, or at worst to be found on later pages. It may be hard to identify in the instruction booklet, but the Journal will be full of it, for most reports of research are in essence criticisms of earlier research. For that reason, there will be a good deal of criticism in Asimov as well, although instead of living criticism it will be a report of the criticism of others, which brings in description again.

Notice, however, the nature of what those publications describe and criticize. It is such as to create some kind of parity between writer and reader. What the reporter describes on page one is what any of us might describe if we had enjoyed the opportunity provided the reporter by the nature of his occupation. What the chief surgeon at Such-and-such Hospital criticizes in the Journal any of us might criticize most effectively after a dozen years or so in medical research. I do not say that in either instance we would necessarily describe or criticize as sensibly and efficiently as those who actually do so, or that opportunities to describe or criticize for a wide and interested audience are readily come by. But those are not questions of form but questions of better and worse. The central point is that what is being described and criticized is external to those who do the description and the criticism, and is therefore available in principle for any of us who might wish to tackle it.

That characteristic constitutes the distinction between expository writing and what more often than not goes by the name *creative* writing, the second of the two broad families of the written word. Creative is precisely what it is, for in one way or another the world with which it deals is invented by the writer himself. To be sure, it is a world that may come to have a kind of existence of its own; certainly the Denmark of <u>Hamlet</u> is a good deal more real to most of us than the hard physical Denmark lying between the Netherlands and Norway. But it is not the hard physical Denmark at all, as Shakespeare pointed out elsewhere in the canon when he spoke of poets who bestow on "airy nothing/A local habitation and a name."

For better or for worse, almost all poets and a good many playwrights and novelists and short story writers and a few of their kin at MGM and CBS are creative writers. So, to some extent, are diarists and investigative journalists unless they chance to be honest, which some of them are. Indeed, the world is full of creative writers, against whom society as a whole protects itself by placing enormous barriers between the act of writing and the act of publication.

Leaving the poets aside, these writers, too, deal for the most part in description and criticism. But what they are describing is for the most part bred within their own imaginations and brought into existence by the act of writing, abetted in some instances by the act of performance. The criticism, too, is derived from the imagination of the writer, for the world he criticizes is by and large a world he has brought into being for exactly that purpose.

Only the writer himself has direct access to that world. I will be allowed into it as a reader, but not as an observer. I can even describe and criticize the world the writer has brought into being, but then I am on the way to becoming a creative writer myself, for my criticism deals with a world I choose to imagine in place of the world imagined by the writer who inspired me.

In all this, two quite different kinds of activity are involved, however much they may appear to resemble each other. The reporter who describes a baseball game appeals to a real game as his point of reference; the columnist who criticizes his descriptions is expected to refer to that same game. There is no such real world behind the novelist's written word, or the playwright's, or the written word of the critic who puts novelist or playwright in his place.

If this appears to be a derogatory view of creative writing, let me set my own personal record straight. As a writer, I would choose without so much as a moment's hesitation to be the creative writer I am not rather than the expository writer I am. I never had that choice. Leaving aside the question of skills—after all, we have not yet begun to speak of skills—I do not possess in my aggregation of genes and habitudes whatever it may be that goes to constitute a creative writer, and nothing under the sun could endow me with it.

This distinction between the expository writer and the creative writer is not a small matter, and I shall be coming back to it from time to time. It is not of enormous moment for present purposes, but it becomes extremely important when pedagogy is under consideration. For the moment, all that is important is a recognition that the distinction is reasonable.

I find it significant that the distinction between expository and creative writing can be put in terms of the distinction between objective and subjective knowledge, as I can illustrate by a quotation from a book named Objective Knowledge, by that most distinguished philosopher Karl R. Popper. I have abridged it only slightly.

> The most important of human creations, with the most important feedback effects upon ourselves and especially upon our brains, are the higher functions of human language; more especially the *descriptive* function and the *argumentative* function.
> Human languages share with animal languages the two lower functions of language: (1) self-expression and (2) signalling. The self-expressive or symptomatic function of language is obvious: all animal language is symptomatic of the state of some organism. The signalling or release function is likewise obvious: we do not

call any symptom linguistic unless we assume that it can release a response in another organism.

All animal languages and all linguistic phenomena share these two lower functions. But human language has many other functions. Strangely enough, the most important of the higher functions have been overlooked by almost all philosophers. The explanation of this strange fact is that the two lower functions are always present when the higher ones are present, so that it is always possible to "explain" every linguistic phenomenon, in terms of the lower functions, as an "expression" or a "communication."

The two most important higher functions of human languages are (3) the *descriptive* function and (4) the *argumentative* function.

With the descriptive function of human language, the regulative idea of *truth* emerges: that is, of a description which fits the facts.

Further regulative or evaluative ideas are content, truth content, and verisimilitude.

The argumentative function of human language presupposes the descriptive function: arguments are, fundamentally, about descriptions; they criticize descriptions from the point of view of the regulative ideas of truth, content, and verisimilitude. . . .

. . . Without the development of an exosomatic descriptive language . . . there can be *no object* for our critical discussion.

The emphases, in all instances, are Popper's.

It appears to me that what Popper says of language is even more properly to be said of the written word. Those passages underlie in some degree what this book is about. I, for one, do not speak of "higher" and "lower" functions, because I do not find it necessary to do so, and I do not wish to initiate a rank-ordering of the written word in terms of function; I have other fish to fry.

But to the extent that Popper assigns great importance to what he calls the descriptive and the argumentative functions—I generally prefer *critical,* but that is no matter—I am his man. The point he makes is of great significance to his own philosophical views, and applicable in quite another fashion to what I have to say in the chapters that follow.

It is possible that from time to time these paragraphs have aroused fear that I was about to embark upon a consideration of the distinction between writing as art and writing as craft. The fear has been justified, for I am about to do exactly that, and what is worse, do it without much confidence that what I have to say will make much sense. Still, to write about art and make no sense is in the best of traditions.

For better or for worse, I would define a craft to be an activity in which a good deal of confidence can be placed in the relationship between means and ends: so much confidence, indeed, that much of that relationship can be codified. It is possible to acquire an intimate acquaintance with the use of plane and drill and chisel; to say that someone is using them well and someone else is using them badly; and to predict that the one using them well is more likely to achieve whatever it is that both set out to achieve.

In those terms, it is clear that there is a craft of writing, and that some writers are more the masters of their craft than others. There are also worthwhile codifications, some of course better than others, which organize the existing knowledge of the craft: Fowler; Strunk and White. (There are also codifications which are appalling, as might be expected.) There are academic treatises dealing with the proper manipulation of the paragraph or the anatomy of the pluperfect, all of which I am quite willing to consider contributions to the craft, for I am a generous man and not to be swayed by the fact that I have never met a writer who went about his business giving any heed to such treatises.

That there is an art of writing also appears to me indubitable. Certainly, anyone at all can rattle off names of writers whom he considers to be artists, and although no two lists are likely to be exactly the same, it is safe to predict that almost any two lists will have a good many names in common. How to define the achievement of a writer who is acknowledged, over time, to be an artist is quite beyond me. It is clear that he is not doing something *better* than what others are doing and have done, but something *other*. The relationship between the means he adopts and the ends he seeks is almost always obscure, and is certainly obscure at the outset although in the end scholars will ferret some of it out, undeterred by the fact that the artist himself was not ever likely to have given thought to such matters. In any case, the knowledge so laboriously gained is of no consequence at all to a subsequent writer striving to achieve art, since any field of artistic endeavor occupied by a predecessor is closed to him. A composer employing exactly the means Mozart employed and seeking exactly the ends Mozart sought, even though it could be said that he did what Mozart did better than Mozart did it, would be a curiosity but not an artist.

Indeed, it makes some sense to say of art that neither the means employed by an artist nor the ends he seeks are ever entirely clear, however much the effort invested by subsequent analysts. What he achieves becomes art as it becomes somehow transcendent, lying beyond human experience and inexpressible in any terms but its own. That is, in fact, the dilemma of the art critic: if he is analytic he does not in fact deal directly with the art; if he seeks to deal directly with the art he is likely to lapse into a kind of burbling.

In any case, the presence of artistry and craftsmanship in almost all human endeavors is clear enough. The relationship between them is not at all clear. That the craftsman may be an artist seems to me to be beyond a doubt, but it is also clear that he need not be. A craftsman who could duplicate, in all its details, a Chippendale chair would be a pearl beyond price, but its maker no artist, except in the colloquial uses of the word. And that an artist need not be a great craftsman, or indeed any kind of craftsman, seems to me equally clear. To call the James Joyce of Finnegans Wake a craftsman seems to me to be nothing more than a perverse use of the English language; Theodore Dreiser was hard put to write a coherent sentence; at the very top of the heap, a great many of

Shakespeare's sentences are grammatical nightmares and more than a few have no determinable meaning. But of course Joyce was not proposing to write elegant prose; Dreiser's mind was not on syntax; Shakespeare was trying to say more than the language could possibly handle, and even managed to do so.

In short, whether the craftsman is also an artist or the artist also a craftsman seems to me to be a question without significant meaning. Any given practitioner may be one, or the other, or both, or neither. But he cannot presume to be an artist and ask that he be judged on the criteria of a craftsman, or a craftsman and demand he be judged on the criteria of an artist. There was an architect not many years back who designed a most expensive home, the interior of which stabilized at 100 degrees Fahrenheit during the summer and was so designed that it could not be cooled. "Let them live outside," he said, when that fact was pointed out to him. If anywhere a Hell is being planned for such craftsmen, I will be happy to put up some of the venture capital.

But that is by the by. What I wish to come to, in the end, is the flat statement that I shall be dealing exclusively with the written word as a craft, and with the writer as a craftsman. I would not want that to suggest I am unaware that writing may also be treated as an art, and its writer as an artist. I simply do not intend to treat them that way, partly because I have no taste for it and partly because I honestly do not believe it is a useful thing to do. But that is a quite different matter, and can be argued out in another place, although not by me.

I will be proceeding on the assumption that the spoken word is prior to the written word, in every sense. It is not a particularly bold assumption, since I find it most difficult to believe that anyone would be willing to debate the point. The whole matter is somewhat more complicated than might immediately appear, and has its own ramifications, with which we will be obliged to deal. But one aspect of it is worth a slight tack to starboard even during this runup, because it is central to my own view of the written word and I want to have it out in the clear as quickly as possible. I refer to speech that remains unspoken. That sounds too paradoxical for comfort, and I plan to employ a locution about which I am slightly uneasy although it may be quite legitimate: I shall call it here and hereafter *unvoiced speech*, shuddering slightly each time I do so.

If you stop to think about it—and there I have you. Stop to think about almost anything at all and you are likely to discover, if you step back a bit, that you are talking to yourself. For most people most of the time and for all people some of the time, ordinary everyday thinking is associated with unvoiced speech. It is an instance not of one central nervous system establishing communication with another, but of a central nervous system establishing communication with itself, and language is the symbol system it employs for the purpose.

Not always. Crossing the street against traffic, you are not likely to think verbally but kinematically, creating images of your own possible movements and those of the approaching vehicles, calculating consequences with the use of neither words nor numbers, and acting accordingly. It is possible and not even very difficult to think visually or dynamically or musically. At the extreme, Einstein maintained that he never thought in words at all, until it became necessary to prepare his hypotheses for publication. I find that extremely difficult to believe, for his letters and his occasional writing display a magnificent prose style. But he was a very honest man, and so I must.

But most of us talk to ourselves, and indeed would not be able to go about our daily affairs if we did not. Unvoiced speech continues minute by minute, hour by hour, through all the waking day and into our dreams. That is not a statement that can be easily checked, for the moment you begin to introspect you find you are talking to yourself, and there is no easy way around it. It is simply impossible for most of us to not-think and examine ourselves not-thinking. Perhaps someday, with the right assortment of electrodes in the right tangles of the brain. But not yet.

When I speak of *thinking,* by the way, I do not necessarily have anything particularly grand in mind. For the moment, I allude only to one of the several characteristics that distinguish us from the trailing arbutus.

The intimate relationship between language and thought led not too long ago to a school which said (presumably to itself as well as to the world at large) that thinking was nothing but unvoiced speech, and that was that. Its guru was John Watson, and in order to make his theory as coherent as a healthy theory ought to be, Dr. Watson was obliged to maintain that all thoughts were accompanied by imperceptible movements of the muscles associated with voiced speech. Since they were imperceptible, Dr. Watson could not very well prove they were there, but by the same token no one else could prove they were not, which made for an impregnable if somewhat dim theory. It reappears from time to time in much modified forms.

In some ways, I myself respect unvoiced speech much as others respect Broken English; it has a richness all its own. I for one have never dared use the word *farrago* in conversation, because for the life of me I have never been able to pronounce it confidently. In unvoiced speech I can more or less mumble it, and I use it all the time. Used it when I read (to myself) this paragraph, as a matter of fact.

The subject is worth consideration in its own right, but it would take us much too far from the matter at hand. I have introduced it here because it is of great significance in any consideration of the written word, and it had better be on the agenda from the outset. Where it is now firmly fixed, I trust.

Chapter Two

The Burden

Polonius. What do you read, my lord?
Hamlet. Words, words, words.

WILLIAM SHAKESPEARE, Hamlet

IF WE CAN AGREE that the craft of the written word is worth thinking about, we can plunge ahead into the difficult business of doing just that. We are in a position no different from that of other honest craftsmen; we are obliged to become acquainted with the material with which we are going to work, which is our native language. I regret to say that we shall find it to be most intractable material, and we are better off facing that cruel fact from the outset.

Let us consider some unexceptionable English word, and to be completely fair about it select a word concerning which it might seem that a meeting of the minds is pretty much inescapable whether it is to be employed in conversation or in the act of written composition. A noun might very well serve our purposes, since on the face of it nouns—or some of them—are what we employ to represent those aspects of our immediate surroundings that we can point at, thereby dispensing with language altogether.

13

After all, if the object is at hand we have no great need for a symbol with which to represent it. Obviously this is only occasionally the case, which may be why early man felt the need to invent language in the first place.

Nouns, to be sure, have come a long way since then, but I suspect it is still true that in principle at least they symbolize what might grossly be denominated "things." That simple fact is a matter of great torment for philosophers, since for reasons which have never been entirely clear to me it seems to have led them, at one time or another, to believe that the act of saying "mermaid" confers some sort of reality upon the existence of mermaids. This is of no great moment when mermaids are under discussion, but it can be most confusing if what is being considered is *justice.* We will be having at matters such as these as we go along, but not just now.

We shall resist the temptation to speak of justice or even mermaids, and restrict ourselves to as uncomplicated a word as we can possibly find: the word *bread.* It is a word that exists within all the languages with which most of us are at all familiar, although I can conceive of a culture which does not possess it. If ever there was a word possessing hard edges, *bread* should be it. As a symbol, it is of course intended to call to mind the object it symbolizes, for it is of no great use otherwise.

It is obvious and not at all disconcerting to recognize that as a practical matter it generally calls to mind not an object but an indistinctly conceived family of objects. When a waitress in an unfamiliar restaurant announces, "I'll bring the bread and butter right away," you cannot possibly visualize exactly what it is that will arrive at your table some ten minutes later. Some rolls, perhaps, or several slices of pumpernickel, or an imaginative mixture of obscure chemicals wrapped in cellophane and labeled "Melba Toasties." By general agreement and in the absence of adjectives and adverbs, these all go by the name of "bread," which as a general matter is as it should be.

At the same time, the same word *bread* spoken in surroundings with which we are entirely familiar has a quite different meaning. In a restaurant to which one returns with frequency or in a home of the old-fashioned nuclear kind the word *bread* is extremely well defined, and what it calls to mind differs very little among those who eat there often. If the restaurant, for example, is in the custom of serving crusty rolls (and I dearly wish that more of them did so), the waiter, generally male in that sort of restaurant, may once in a long while come to the table bearing a heaping basket of super-market bread and announce, "The bread never got here today." No one will be confused.

Clearly, there is great economy in such employment of the language. What I have said, briefly summarized, is that the word *bread* refers in one instance to a well-defined object, and in an-other to a family of such objects which is a good deal less well-defined. The ambiguity that results is not particularly disconcert-ing, most of the time, but it is there none the less. Returning once again to the restaurant that serves crusty hard rolls whenever the delivery system does not fail, the words "I'll bring you the bread right away" mean one thing to me and another thing to my friend from out of town. The matter is resolved when the bread arrives. No harm done, at least as far as language is concerned, although it may well turn out that my friend detests hard crusty rolls.

In matters of great importance to a society, words are likely to be sharply defined whenever sharp definition is possible. For an American, the word *snow* used in isolation signifies a great family of meteorological or meteorologically produced phenomena, ranging all the way from a violent blizzard to a heap of cold wet mud in a big-city gutter. The languages of the Eskimos, we are told, contain specific words for each of those states of affairs and for several dozen others as well, all of which we would be normally content to call simply "snow." The Eskimos are not aware of this, any more than most Americans are aware that they possess and employ at least as many different words for "automobile" as the Eskimos employ for "snow."

It becomes tempting to look upon all this as further illustration of evolutionary efficiency, since man managed to develop, without thinking much about it, language systems which included both precise words and family words, using them in turn as convenience might dictate. While that is a fair description of artificial languages and of a good many variants of English, it does not apply in any sense to natural languages. American English possesses a hundred words for "automobile" where the Eskimos may possess but one, not so that the language may be more precise but so that it may be a little less vague. Each of those hundred words itself bears a whole family of meanings. To say "I own an import" is less vague than to say "I own an automobile," but spoken by one person it may well signify a Datsun and by another a Mercedes.

Indeed, it is difficult to believe that any word in the natural language is entirely precise, although some are a good deal more precise than others. The best way to make this clear is to move outside one natural language, such as one version or another of the English language, into a second and somewhat different natural language. My personal history chances to make it most convenient for me to deal with French, but any Western European language will do and indeed I am quite certain that any natural language at all would do, although obviously I cannot really know that.

The French word *pain* will almost invariably be translated into English as *bread,* except by an extremely sophisticated translator. As a practical matter, *pain* is a nutriment produced by exposing to moderate heat over a moderate period of time a mixture of elements which can be relied upon to include a cereal of some kind and water; which will generally include salt and yeast; and beyond that can include pretty nearly anything under the sun provided that the resulting product is a solid which can be cut or broken, and which will not immediately poison the eater. This crude description—not definition—of *pain* is also a crude description of *bread,* and accordingly the first entry under *pain* in any French-English dictionary (and the only entry in a highly abridged French-English dictionary) will be *bread,* and the first entry under *bread* in an English-French dictionary will be *pain.* All very tidy.

But it takes no great effort of introspection for me to realize that what presents itself to my mind when I hear or read the French word *pain* bears only a crude resemblance to what presents itself when I hear the word *bread*.

(It is my misfortune that *pain* has an English meaning that has absolutely nothing to do with bread. Fortunately, what I actually hear sounds French and not English, so at least *I* am not confused.)

To put the matter in its simplest terms, a good deal of what comes to mind when I hear the French word *pain* is broadly speaking an image of what is likely to follow whenever I might say "Du pain, s'il vous plaît," or something of that general sort. Quite obviously, only in the most general terms does that coincide with what happens when I say "Bread, please." In those two instances I receive quite different products, designed in part for quite different purposes. I can make a sandwich of *bread* if I choose, but it is most difficult to make a reasonable sandwich of *pain*. Indeed, I can make my point in a most forceful way, though idiosyncratic: in practice I eat about as much *pain* as I can lay my hands on, including even the imitation *pain* that is occasionally to be found in extremely expensive French restaurants in such cities as New York and New Orleans, whereas I eat virtually no *bread* at all. This is not merely Francophilia, since I can honestly say that I eat a good deal more *steak* than *bifteck* and drink more *coffee* than *café,* for exactly the same general reasons.

Yet even that does nothing more than scratch the surface. When I say "Bread, please," I set up reverberations in my mind of which I may not be conscious. The word *bread* as well as the product "bread" exists in my experience in its own right, and that existence is in some instances very rich. It exists as a part of the sentence "Give us this day our daily bread," which may have a world of connotations that have nothing at all to do with nutrition or sandwiches. It exists also as part of similar sentences or phrases, such as "bread cast upon waters" and "takes the bread out of my mouth" (which is associated with the current meaning of *bread* in American slang) and "it's bread and butter to him" and how many others I do not know. It exists in intimate association with memories in which the bread itself, or the word *bread,* plays only a trivially small part. (I have extremely strong memories of an afternoon in Amana, Iowa . . . but no matter.)

All these varieties of experience converge whenever the *bread* is uttered in my presence or when I encounter it written. Whether I am fully conscious of the associations, or conscious of them at all, has relatively little to do with the case. It is, in fact, just those experiences that determine for me the meaning of the word in all its richness, and the connection between that meaning and whatever it is that Webster happens to say is really not of very much significance at all.

If I turn to the French word *pain,* however, I find myself suddenly impoverished. Despite the years I have lived in France, the word itself remains comparatively bare of associations. There is a line of poetry in which François Villon speaks of the plight of the poverty-stricken in the Paris of his century, and writes: "Et pain ne voyent qu'aux fenestres." I understand each word in that line, but the line itself I do not understand at all in the sense that any educated Frenchman must understand it, and even the least educated Frenchman must somehow feel it. I simply do not have the complex of experiences, directly and vicariously, in the real world and in the world of literature, that is necessary to wrench from those simple words the depth of emotion that Villon managed somehow to write into them.

For just those reasons the process of translation from one language into another as it is imposed upon us during our years of formal schooling, useful as it may be as a tactic, conveys no more than the bare surface of what we ought to be hearing in the foreign language. To be adequate, a translator must possess a profound knowledge of both languages, and more than that, be able to summon it up at will, which is the hard part. The title of Marcel Proust's monumental novel, or novels, is À la Recherche du Temps Perdu, which any grammarian will tell you means "in search of lost time." The translator who had the genius to carry the meaning rather than the words into English called it <u>Remembrance of Things Past,</u> and thereby enriched the title with all the overtones of a great Shakespearean sonnet. As I have said, I really can never know what "à la recherche du temps perdu" means to a Frenchman, but I have faith enough in that translator to believe that it means what "remembrance of things past" means to me, as nearly as may be, which I regret to say is not very nearly.

Wherever it counts, the connotations within a language supersede the denotations. The French phrase "tête-à-tête" is a precise counterpart, word for word, of the English phrase "head to head." Yet the first has romantic overtones, and calls up images of lovers in a dimly lit restaurant; the second suggests a confrontation with a bull in a small enclosed corral.

But all that is even more complex a matter than any determination of the meaning of *bread* or *pain.* As far as I am concerned, the meaning of *bread* is a summation of all the experiences I have had, directly with substances I choose to call "bread" and indirectly with other people's use of the word, including its use in literature and in song. To the extent that the totality of my experience differs from the totality of the experience of others, as it absolutely must, the meaning carried by that word when I use it or when I hear it is unique. Whoever you may be, I do not mean by *bread* exactly what you mean by *bread,* although as a practical matter our experiences are enough alike so that differences in meaning will be encountered only out on the margins.

There are, however, instances in which I cannot rely upon a commonality of experience. They are most important when abstractions are involved: conceptualizations rather than things. Consider, for example, such words as *justice* or *honor* or *truth* or *beauty.* It is a commonplace that words such as those rarely mean quite the same thing to different people. What I am asserting here is that they cannot possibly mean the same thing to any two people, and even more strongly cannot have a meaning which is common to any group of people; even that the problem in such instances lies not at the margin but at the very core.

It is not the fact of ambiguity that should concern us. It is the inevitability of ambiguity, and the fact that it lies in the nature of language and cannot be resolved. If I were to seek to replace the word *justice,* with all its ambiguity, I would be reduced finally to recount the totality of all my experience that bears upon what I now call "justice." I cannot do that in the first instance because most of those experiences lie beyond my power of recollection, and in the second instance because my account would necessarily be rendered in language itself ambiguous, although a good deal less ambiguous than *justice,* and most of all because no one would put up with such a recital.

I spoke earlier of language as a set of symbols by means of which one central nervous system communicates with another. It lies in the nature of what we generally mean by "central nervous system" that the communication can at best be approximate. There is no point at all in trying to render it exact. There is a good deal of point in trying to render it as exact as possible, which is what sooner or later we will be dealing with. Meanwhile we must know our enemy, which is language. To know it, fortunately, is to love it.

Let me repeat clearly the consequences of what I have been saying, distasteful as they may be. There is a sense in which there are as many languages as there are speakers, and it follows (in terms more relevant to my own concerns as I write all this) as many English languages as there are those who speak anything at all that one would be willing to call English.

It is clear that we are in a real tangle at this moment. Obviously you can turn my own argument against me, and simply say, wearily or anxiously or furiously, as the mood may be on you, "That is not what I mean by the word *language.*" Which is, after all, exactly my point.

I could, of course, respond that it is my book and like Humpty Dumpty in Through the Looking-Glass—who is really the last word on the subject—I intend words in this book to mean exactly what I want them to mean. (Lewis Carroll, after all, was a mathematician.) Alternatively, I suppose I might preen myself on having made a good case, and leave the matter there.

But I am much more comfortable saying that as a practical matter those views on language—or that usage of the word *language,* if you prefer—are useful to a person who is interested in the craft of expository prose. For him, ambiguity is the enemy, above all others, and "know thine enemy" is sound tactical advice. He battles against ambiguity with every ounce of his being, and he always loses. But the battle must go on, and he must hope to win an engagement now and then.

It is a battle he cannot avoid. An editor may tell him that his book or essay or report is ill-conceived, in which case he can stand his ground and argue the matter out. A reader may call it indecent or untimely or dull or just plain wrongheaded, and again he can fight back as he may choose. His wife or mistress or creditor may ask why he does not find better uses for his time, and he may demur in any way that is open to him. But the critic, whatever his status, who simply says to him, "I did not understand that sentence," has him by the heels, because there is absolutely nothing that can be said in response, and absolutely nothing that can be done but rewrite the sentence.

The alternative is to abandon expository writing and become a mathematician. Well, I never tried, but it wouldn't have worked out.

Chapter Three

The Task

Who casts to write a living line, must sweat.

BEN JONSON, "To the Memory of My Beloved,
the Author, William Shakespeare"

I HAVE BEEN at great pains to stress the ambiguity of natural language, for the most part in terms of the performed or the spoken word but by implication of the written word as well. At the same time, I have specified that my interest, as I write this, lies in the employment of the written word for purposes of description and criticism, and at another level the employment of the written word as an instrument that is very nearly essential if any kind of organized thinking is to take place. Those two quite different aspects of language do not make particularly good neighbors. It is clear that description is not likely to be of much use if it does not clearly describe, and that criticism is not going to move matters forward unless he who is criticized has a clear understanding of the nature of the criticism. In neither instance is the task an easy one, which is not to call it impossible.

There is an obligation to provide within the dialogue what I shall call lucidity. The best I can do in the way of definition is borrow a notion from communications theory and related arcane activities: the notion of "noise in the system." What is generally called "static" in a radio transmission or occasionally a telephone conversation is exactly that; in television transmission it is likely to be distortion of one kind or another in the picture that is received, but it is none the less called "noise." Its characteristic is that the message received differs from the message transmitted because of deficiencies in the transmission system or events that penetrate the system from without. Lucidity, then, means the absence of such noise, and nothing more.

In that sense, it has nothing directly to do with meaning. The most lucid communication in the world may be completely meaningless, or may contain a multitude of meanings. The man who, upon being introduced to a neighbor's newborn infant, remarks, "That's a baby!" is being as lucid as the language allows, but the meaning that the proud parent assigns to his comment is the business of the proud parent and not of the speaker.

In the spirit of Humpty Dumpty, however, I propose to extend the definition of "lucidity" somewhat, and include within it the broader notion of ambiguity. To return to the analogy above, I shall consider ambiguity to be "noise in the system" on equal footing with all the other noises that perturb communication.

I must sooner or later be more precise in specifying the load I expect to impose upon the words *lucid* and *lucidity,* but it is something that must be permitted to develop as we go along. There is nothing unusual about that, for as a matter of general practice we generate our language in just that fashion. We have quite enough to carry us for a while, for the direction in which we are proceeding must be clear enough for the business at hand.

Clear enough, at least, as long as I am content to deal strictly with expository prose. So far as the creative writer is concerned, ambiguity is certainly not noise, and in some instances ambiguity is what he most earnestly seeks. I adduce the character of Mercutio in Romeo and Juliet—he is a favorite character of mine and pretty obviously of Shakespeare as well, and had to be killed early in the play if the play was to remain <u>Romeo and Juliet</u> and not become <u>Mercutio and Friends</u>. In the play as written, he is stabbed during his attempt to keep the peace, and solicitously asked how badly wounded he believes himself to be. He thereupon replies, " 'tis not so deep as a well, nor so wide as a church door, but 'tis enough, 'twill serve."

In the restricted sense, it is a thoroughly lucid reply. But at the same time, it clearly cannot mean what it says. His solicitous friends were not asking whether his wound was as wide as a church door, for having at one time or another seen both church doors and Mercutio, they sensed no particular need to pose any such question.

But Mercutio's reply echoes and reechoes in the ear, as Shakespeare intended, and has done so for some four hundred years. "Deep" and "well" and "church" and "door" all resonate with notions of death: resonate strongly for some of us and weakly for others, and what they call up within the central nervous system to which I so often recur is different for each man and woman who reads or hears the lines. "Enough" and "serve," and the weariness of the repetitive form in which they are employed, carry with them the notion of acceptance. What Mercutio has actually said is "I am dying," but he has said it without mention of the word "die" and said it in a manner that moves each one of us in the fashion which for him is most powerful.

On the face of it, of course, the sentence in question had a meaning which is entirely accessible, and the ambiguity is overlaid on that surface meaning. I myself cannot say the same of the following:

THE EMPEROR OF ICE-CREAM

Call the roller of big cigars,
The muscular one, and bid him whip
In kitchen cups concupiscent curds.
Let the wenches dawdle in such dress

As they are used to wear, and let the boys
Bring flowers in last month's newspapers.
Let be be the finale of seem.
The only emperor is the emperor of ice-cream.

Take from the dresser of deal,
Lacking the three glass knobs, that sheet
On which she embroidered fantails once
And spread it so as to cover her face.
If her horny feet protrude, they come
To show how cold she is, and dumb.
Let the lamp affix its beam.
The only emperor is the emperor of ice-cream.

What I have reproduced, quite complete, is a poem by Wallace Stevens. Among those who claim, quite justifiably, that they are expert in matters concerning poetry, Stevens is held to be a poet of real significance. Not in the very top rank, to be sure, but near enough, and certainly a poet not to be scorned. The poem in question is not merely a false start, or sixteen lines written by the poet on an off day and, after limited consideration, pitched out. It is part of the Stevens canon, and has been published and republished.

I acknowledge without shame that it makes no sense to me at all, although there is not a single word that I do not understand, with the possible exception of "fantail," which may in this context (if a context can be found) have a meaning other than that with which I am familiar. I have no idea what the poem as a whole is intended to signify, and now that I have read it half a dozen times I find that I really do not care. I am quite willing to concede that this may very well indicate some serious inadequacy of my own, and I suspect that English departments in every major university can direct me to an authority on Stevens, or at the worst on modern American poetry, who would be willing to tell me so, quite forcefully. Well, if those who are in charge of the care and feeding of poetry maintain that those sixteen lines are an authentic sample of the genus "poem," I will offer no resistance. It is their business, and I am quite willing to assume that they know what they are talking about. If they add that they find the poem lucid enough for all normal purposes, I might find substance for a quarrel but would never press it. But I cannot concede that it is unambiguous, and if I were to address myself to two experts in modern American poetry instead of merely one expert, that fact would immediately emerge. If pressed, however, they might well agree that in its ambiguity lies its strength.

Thinking in terms of expository prose, I would not wish to call those lines lucid. I propose to preserve that word for written material which is maximally accessible to the reader, and such prose must be minimally ambiguous. The task, clearly, is to find means of making expository prose lucid (in those terms) when the language in which it is cast is itself inevitably ambiguous. What is involved is craftsmanship, directed toward an end we are beginning to define: lucidity. That it is a craft in which Stevens was probably not very much interested is neither here nor there, for Stevens had other ends in view, and the question in his case is whether his craftsmanship was up to those ends. I am quite sure that I could become interested in that question, and others like it, but not here.

Because I am sensitive on the matter, I feel obliged to insist I am not suggesting for one moment some kind of hierarchy of the written word, in which writing that is not entirely lucid is to be despised or even merely deprecated in favor of writing that is. As a purely personal matter, I would far rather be capable of "creative writing" than of the craft I actually exercise, but I see no reason why my personal preference should enter into any scale of values one way or another. The hard truth, as I have said, is that the choice between the two does not lie in my hands but in my genes, and there is nothing on earth or in heaven that could make a useful creative writer out of the raw material of which I am composed. Pity.

I submit extracts from three books and the like, all written by Americans for other Americans to read:

This conflict between the circuits, however, does not require plenary consideration because the points upon which the two circuit courts disagreed have already been decided in *Manhart.* In our brief *amicus curiae* in support of the petition in *Peters,* the AAUP and other *amici* suggested that an appropriate decision there would be to grant the petition and reverse summarily on the strength of *Manhart.* If the Court adopts that suggestion the instant petition should be denied.

Although, by hindsight, one can view the works of Bloch and Mumford on the kernel of the Albanese map as a discussion of K^0 in algebraic geometry, the real starting point of this topic was Bloch's formula expressing the Chow ring of a projective variety in K-theoretic terms, proved in full generality by Quillen. More recent, and promising, developments are Bloch's attempts to associate to elliptic function fields an analogue of the higher regulators known in the K-theory of number fields, and work on K_3 and the dilogarithm function.

05450	Cursup	LD	A, (DWNCUR)
05460		AND	A
05470		JR	Z (CONTU1)
05480		DEC	A$
05490		LD	(DOWNCUR), A
05500		RET	
05510			
05520	CONTU1	LD	A, (LSTARW)

The first of those three strange extracts is from a legal brief presented to the Supreme Court of the United States. It is incomprehensible to any but those familiar in some detail with the matters being litigated, and it contains terms and usages that are found nowhere in the language except in documents prepared by and for lawyers. All the same, there is no doubt that it is written in the English language. If one is willing to take account of the fact that the rules of the game absolutely demand that it be written in jargon, it is not at all badly written; I could have been a good deal more extreme in my selection.

The second extract is part of a description of work being under-taken by mathematicians at the Institute for Advanced Study. Again, it is English, but a shadow of doubt creeps in. It may be that no more than a few hundred people in the entire world are capable of reading and understanding that modest paragraph, and the oddest aspect of all is that a good proportion of that number do not know the English language at all, for the universal jargon of mathematical writing is so dense that it really matters very little what language it is written in.

The third extract comes from a magazine dealing with computers. It is written in what is called assembly language, which is a kind of transition language between (in this instance) English and the language that a computer can understand, itself called machine language. Although traces of English can readily be detected in assembly language, it is clearly an artificial language.

The succession of extracts can be characterized in another fashion. The three "languages," if for the moment they may be called that, are progressively less copious. Anything at all can be said in the language of the law, although no sane man tries, since only legal matters can be said well. The language of the second abstract, on the other hand, is so finely tuned toward mathematics that it can be used for little but mathematics or pseudomathematics. (There is a good deal more of the latter than of the former, but that is something else again.) The third extract, finally, is in a language that can say remarkably few things in a remarkably narrow context. Indeed, as it stands it can do nothing but give instructions to one particular kind of silicon chip. There are, as I recall it, some seven hundred such instructions, and that is the end of the language.

Include the language in which this book is being written, and it is clear just what is taking place. It is possible to add precision to a language, but only at the price of limiting the capacity of the language to deal with the full range of experience. From the lawyer to the mathematician to the computer scientist, the language becomes less and less ambiguous, and less and less generally useful. The natural language is always ambiguous, and never entirely precise, which is in fact extremely useful, since most of what we want to say is not very precise, either. "I must always be very careful," Niels Bohr once said, "never to speak more clearly than I think." It was a wise remark, but beyond a certain point the language itself protects us.

I intend to deal exclusively with natural language. This will involve a certain amount of iconoclasm, since I do believe that the language which appears in grammars and other such plague spots within the educational system deals not with the natural language but with a highly artificial language created primarily to make life easier for teachers and harder for students. It has taken a good many years for me to rid myself of the haunting memory of the pluperfect, and I do not intend to become reacquainted.

It is possible to look upon all this as a suggestion that the very concept of an English language is open to question, but that, too, would be a nonsensical position for a sane man to adopt. The difficulties lie in determining its status. The outcome of such a determination has a profound effect upon the attitude an individual adopts when he stops to think about his language qua language.

The tendency, most widely represented among English teachers and those who write about the language in the periodical press, is to adopt what might be called the Platonic view. Such a view asserts that there exists in some realm or another The English Language in a state of marmorial perfection and ineffable bliss, and that what we actually observe and employ is a form of that ideal English language corrupted by reason of our own brutish state. There is on the other hand a somewhat more crass view, which asserts that certain acquired habits will be called English and certain others will not, and that at the margins the matter of who calls what which is subject to personal taste and in any event doesn't really make much difference. Usually.

The first of those two attitudes clearly encourages and indeed is inseparable from the notion of a "correct" English, which we are thereupon exhorted to attain. By the definition incorporated in that attitude we are not going to attain it, and the best we can do in practice is pay close attention and strive. More often than not, we are encouraged to pay scrupulous attention to etymology, although the relevance of origins to usage is dubious at best, and too much homage to etymology would rob us of such useful words as *superstitious*, although *supercilious* stands up quite well. Recourse to earlier usage is also called upon when it serves the caller's purpose, although even so simple a word as *nice* seems to have meant almost anything at all at one time or another. It is also good form to appeal to one or another dead language, although before languages die they pose all the problems that English now poses. But we are commanded to eschew the split infinitive for no better reason than the fact, if it is a fact, that in Latin it was impossible to split an infinitive just as in English it is impossible to split an adverb. (I refer here only to the written language, since in the spoken language the word "absogoddamlutely" is neither unheard of nor unheard, and a stronger variant is available.)

Alternatively, we are gravely adjured to adopt the language of the "cultured" among us, which generally signifies the language of the man or woman who is offering the adjuration. And at the extreme, sheer inspiration generates dogma of one kind or another, as when John Simon brilliantly invents a distinction between "each other" and "one another" which has never been known to exist and which cannot be justified by etymology, or the history of usage, or an appeal to Greek or Latin, but amounts merely to the assertion that Simon has gained privileged access to The English Language.

I trust I have made it clear that I have no admiration for the Platonic view. It does, however, provide a discipline that my own views of the nature of language do not offer. I am quite persuaded that some forms of English usage are better than others, but I am required to make the case for that belief instance by instance, and it is not always easy. I envy those who are at home with the true religion and enjoy acolytes in attendance at the shrine, much as a physician must from time to time envy the faith healer. And the excesses aside, those who worship with the John Simons tend to speak and write better English than those who do not, if only because they are paying attention. All the same, the attitude repels me.

It is not comfortable to face the fact that a language has no fixed structure and its important words have no fixed meaning. Yet neither the written word nor the language itself can be comprehended on any other basis. Above all, if the language were otherwise it would not meet our needs. It would cease to be a means by which one central nervous system can communicate with another. Language is a contingent phenomenon, amenable to the requirements of a contingent universe. It would not otherwise be useful.

The sum of it is that the lawyer and the mathematician and the scientist—and the bridge player, for all that—can make systematic attempts to push ambiguity far out into the margin, but in doing so they suffer grievously. For one thing, although they increment the lucidity with which they address each other, they forfeit some of their ability to address others about matters which are of great significance to them unless they have the strength of will to abandon their private language when they are outside the guild. It ought not be difficult to do so, but it is. What is far more serious, however, is that they impose severe limits upon themselves, for as long as the lawyer talks or writes the private language of the law, he can talk or write of nothing but the law, for his language will not permit him to do so. Legal jargon does not even fit the universe of the law as neatly as the lawyer would like it to, and the universe of the law is a tiny little universe indeed.

I have defined lucidity in a fashion that suits my purposes, and I shall find it necessary to sharpen that definition as we go forward. Language is a human creation and thinking a human activity heavily dependent upon language. Writing and speaking must forever compromise between utility and precision; a language that was perfectly precise would come very close to being perfectly useless.

Lucidity is the product of a craft which, like any other craft, must be content with making the most of the materials with which it deals. Craftsmanship can be studied and learned. Some will surely learn it better than others, but there is an inevitability about that, too, and there is little profit in concerning oneself about inevitabilities. And it is a craft well worth learning.

We can now get on with our business, which is that of trying to gain a greater understanding of the craft we had better learn, and go on learning, if we are to call ourselves craftsmen.

Chapter Four

Looking Backward

Since our concern was speech, and speech impelled us
To purify the dialect of the tribe
And urge the mind to aftersight and foresight . . .

T. S. ELIOT, "Little Gidding"

AFTER all this time spent demonstrating that no natural language lends itself to lucid discourse, we are fully prepared to enter into the search for lucidity. I cannot at this moment recall whether Jason managed to find the golden fleece or returned home fleeceless, but in any event it was worth looking for and I have no doubt that he gained something for all his effort.

The place to begin is at the beginning and at the lowest possible level. The very beginning, since it must have occurred several hundred million years ago, give or take several hundred million, is necessarily lost to us. Most animals signal by means of noises, as anyone may find out simply by kicking the nearest dog. Bees, they tell us, can even give each other directions, like an insect AAA, without making any noises at all. In short, among organisms which possess any reasonably elaborate central nervous system, some capacity to communicate by means of symbols of one kind or another can be expected.

But only in man does that symbol system extend beyond the present moment and instant necessity. Only man can make noises signifying "I intend to" or "I did" or "I will" (although a dog can say "I won't," which, unlike "I will," is a response to what the dog at least construes as an instant need). Whether man has this capacity because he possesses so admirable a vocal system, or whether he possesses that vocal system because the species found it to be of survival value, I shall leave to the evolutionists. Or to shift ground a bit and put it in Popper's terms, train a chimpanzee as you may, he cannot describe and he cannot argue or criticize except to the extent that a nasty bite can be looked upon as argument and criticism.

What was constructed in a given human (or humanoid, or what you will) society was a mapping of what might be called experience or observation upon distinguishable noises. The experience or observation might relate to the noise-maker's own nervous system or to the large world lying outside his own nervous system. And that mapping, within any given society, was by social agreement: the noises I made to symbolize "hungry" were manifestly noises you would be likely to make if you wished to transmit the same information. If not, they were not particularly useful to either of us.

It appears that the sheer grandeur of that immense social invention has left an indelible mark upon all of us. Nowhere is that mark better represented than in the Bible. There, and in almost all holy writings of the kind, the beginning of language is identified with the creation of the universe. The Gospel According to St. John begins: "In the beginning was the Word," and although that may not mean exactly what St. John had in mind, it is what the King James translators had in mind when they read the original Greek.

St. John, or the translators (or both), seemed to be going out of their way to make the point, for those opening words flatly contradict the first words of Genesis. "In the beginning," says Genesis, "God created the heaven and the earth." But immediately thereafter, Chapter One of Genesis gives one account of the creation, and Chapter Two generously gives another, and each in its own way stresses language. Having created heaven and earth, "God said Let there be light: and there was light. . . . And God called the light Day." A few lines later, "God called the firmament Heaven," and then "God called the dry land Earth." There is no more naming in Chapter One: the rest seems to have been left to mankind.

Chapter Two has God turn lexicography over to Adam: "And out of the ground the Lord God formed every beast of the field, and every fowl of the air; and brought them unto Adam to see what he would call them; and whatsoever Adam called every living creature, that was the name thereof."

This identification of name with creation haunts us still. To some extent, most of us look upon our own names as guarantors of our own existence. We do not readily give it to strangers; we tear up bits of paper on which it is printed or written, and each time we hear it we seem to enjoy a reassurance that after all we really are.

It makes a certain amount of sense. No one can think about me without possessing some kind of symbol that identifies me, and far more often than not that symbol is my name or some other set of words such as "that disagreeable man in the corner." Even I, thinking about myself, seem to need the word *me* or *myself* to set me off as an object of thought. If I am not named or cannot be "named," I cannot be thought about—and if I am not and cannot be thought about, do I really exist? But as I have repeatedly noted, there are tangles of this kind whenever we deal with language—this tangle is about the meaning of the word *exist*—and I shall not say any more about it.

It is all speculative, of course, but the earliest words—if I may use the word *word* without formally introducing it—were probably imitative, or onomatopoeic if we must be formal. The noise for "gurgle" probably sounds like gurgling even in most highly developed languages. And probably there was initially no pattern in the movement toward the arbitrary symbol, although there is generally a kind of pattern today when new words are invented. It must have been a slow drift that took place over millennia, and that drift took different paths in different societies. But this is far more than I know, or than anyone else knows, although there are no doubt many more qualified to guess than I am.

Of all the inventions man has ever made, this was by far the most consequential. Indeed, it is misleading to write that man made it, since it is far more sensible to say that the invention made man, and was indeed "the creation." I am not now being religious, however, and this particular version of creationism would not be acceptable to the Moral Majority.

Like most inventions, it was not completed at the first stroke. Noises, however skillfully they may be made, are distressingly evanescent. Once the invention took place, the noises could deal with eternity, but noises themselves come and go. They could be repeated, but not stored.

Other symbols were available, of course. A pointed finger served admirably to communicate the same message as noises equivalent to our own "It is over there," and pinching the nostrils clearly indicated "It smells terrible." Nods could signify assent or a smile satisfaction. These were all fine for basic matters, but there was more than that in what men were impelled to communicate, and even those did not pass readily over space and time.

Scratching out a picture on the sand was somewhat more efficient. Indeed, certain gestures were easily scratched: a sketch of the human finger would be sufficient—given some degree of consensus as to its significance—to indicate "We have gone that way." Something of the sort was almost certainly the next step. Sand, of course, lost its messages after the first rain; carving on rock was far better but also far more laborious, but why not? if the message was all that important, or had religious significance, or laid down the law (and lent itself to pictorial treatment). Or clay could be baked. . . .

Those specialists who took over the task of scratching out these signs found it no easy task, and as the signs themselves became conventional there was a natural urge to slop it a bit. The first man to scratch out a pointed finger on rock may very well have taken great pains to scratch out the most realistic pointed finger that his tools and his talents permitted, since it was going to take a mighty act of imagination on the part of the planet's very first literary critic to ferret out the significance of that primitive artifact. After a time, as the habit of scratching out pointed fingers had gained somewhat greater currency, it was accepted by those accustomed to do the scratching and those obliged to puzzle it out that any reasonably straight line, with something on one end to signify direction, would do. The practice had the further advantage that reasonably straight lines are generally a good deal easier to scratch out on intractable material than artistically shaped figures.

But a price had to be paid for this. As the symbols grew in number, the task of keeping them all in mind became more and more onerous. The time came when it was most difficult for the scribe to tend to his reading and writing and still find time to hunt the saber-toothed tiger. It is quite probable that the scribe was the first full-time specialist to emerge in primitive societies, and quite likely that the very nature of his job and the mysteries that came to be associated with it meant also that he was the first priest.

Then, too, the vocabulary was at the outset most limited, and it took still another great leap of the imagination to expand it. Not all the matters that may interest a man, however primitive, lend themselves to the process of straightforward depiction and subsequent stylization. That does quite well for "tiger" but not nearly as well for complex messages or for a code of behavior lately imposed on the society by its current Moses. The wit of man, however, was up to it. It came to be, sooner or later, that scratching out three or four times the stylized symbol that meant "woman," and then the stylized symbol of a full moon, and then three setting suns, would be understood by any respectable scribe to signify that the tribe's ladies' auxiliary would be meeting late in the afternoon three days after the next full moon.

In short, an elaborated symbol system was being created. In principle it had an enormous virtue: if universal agreement could be reached that a certain symbol meant "tiger," it didn't matter a bit how the man who came across that symbol actually said "tiger." The written language was thus divorced from the spoken language, and became a sort of prehistoric Esperanto. Something of that sort happened in China, and to a very large extent persists to this day. It persists in bits and scraps elsewhere as well: a driver who sees ahead of him a signpost bearing a stylized picture of a torch knows he is approaching a school if he speaks English, or une école if he speaks French, or una escuela if he speaks Spanish. Most convenient.

This is all very well when the message to be conveyed is a simple declaration of a simple fact, like "school" or "railroad crossing" or "steep grade ahead." But as a practical matter, to write "as a practical matter" in pictographs makes it necessary to establish some kind of agreement that a picture of a man carrying an umbrella shall mean "practical" (in any language, of course), and that when over time that picture itself has become so stylized that only an expert can trace it back to its origins it will still mean "practical."

And it also means that a man whose natural vocabulary comes to several thousand words is obliged to master several thousand degenerate pictographs if he is to write anything more complex than a recipe, and an utterly bewildering syntax when he is obliged to combine his symbols. It can be done, but only a few have the talent for it, and the task is so demanding that those few rarely have the time or the desire to develop a talent for anything else.

I would be remiss if I did not go into this a bit more closely. I am making much of the fact that a system of stylized pictographs calls for a spoken vocabulary of several thousand words to be represented by a battery of several thousand symbols, more or less. But that spoken vocabulary itself is a battery of several thousand symbols. Indeed, it might appear to be even more complex than the pictograph system, since the pictographs are at least linked, however remotely, to real images and real observations;

except for words like "gurgle" and "hiccup" and "shatter," the spoken vocabulary is linked to nothing at all. It might appear that no more is involved in the use of pictographs than a doubling of effort, which is not trivial but at the same time is not excessive.

Yet it is not the vocabulary itself that is involved in the mastery of the spoken language, but the manner in which that vocabulary is manipulated to create propositions of one kind or another: the syntax. Syntax, and not vocabulary, lies at the heart of communication (which is undeniable), and the syntax of pictographs, where every communication is its own distinct problem, is complexity confounded. The mastery of communication and hence of syntax was of enormous survival value to the scrabbling creatures that grew up over uncounted millennia to be you and me.

Latter-day linguists suggest that evolution, as ordained by Darwin, thus created men and women who are born in possession of a latent mastery of the syntax of spoken language, and no more than a few years of infancy in a minimally supportive environment is all that is necessary to elicit it. (The specifics of the environment, of course, determine whether it will be English or French or a Senegalese dialect that the infant will master.) The written language, in contrast, appeared a mere few thousands of years ago, and evolution has not, or not yet, endowed the infant with any comparable genetic inheritance.

The fact that children learn to speak much as they learn to walk makes the argument persuasive. At the same time . . . The story goes that King James I of England, being persuaded that there was a Natural Language of which all existing languages were degenerate forms, shut up an infant within a prison cell and planned to expose him to no language at all for eleven long years. He would emerge from his isolation, King James assumed, speaking the Natural Language, which the king expected would be Hebrew. The story, at least as I learned it, ends there; I was not told the outcome. I wish I thought the kid did come out speaking Hebrew, in which case I know what I hope he told the king. But in any case, I do sense at least a touch of King James in modern linguistics.

At the same time, I know no better hypothesis. I generally wander back to the fact that the ear is a marvelous instrument, and aside from its services in holding eyeglasses serves but a single function: it hears noises. It hears them all the time, awake or asleep, it hears them over 360 degrees, it cannot be easily turned off, it hears them under virtually all circumstances, none of which can be said of that other remarkable instrument the eye. It also works better than the eye in the newborn infant, although not for long. The child is bathed in noise, immersed in noise, from the moment of birth (and quite possibly even before), and some of that noise is language.

We are, moreover, a communicating species, and parents and others have an overwhelming urge to get in touch with the infant. The amount of effort that is put into teaching the child to speak is staggering; one need only observe the behavior of adults and above all of parents in the presence of an infant. And finally, the child really hasn't very much else to do.

The ease with which adults pick up a foreign language if they are called upon to live in a foreign country is evidence of the role of immersion. Although a certain amount of effort may be invested in the process, most of those who have had the experience would be likely to concede that the return on that effort is trivial, and that the language is learned pretty much without effort in a manner of which the learner is not really conscious. Most never speak it properly, in terms of accent, or copiously, or profoundly, but they all pick up a working vocabulary and a working syntax in a good deal less time than it takes the child to do in his native language. (But of course they have already learned one language or more, and the game at least is familiar.)

But those are speculations. The fact is that of all the symbol systems with which we deal, that of the spoken language is immeasurably easiest to learn. Twenty thousand pictographs and their manipulation is not equivalent to twenty thousand spoken words but perhaps to twenty or thirty times that number. It is so, despite the fact that it is hard to say exactly why.

In any case, we can comprehend a situation where at a given time and place there were two distinct symbolizations of what might be called verbal language, one spoken and one written; one in common use and the other the domain of a small, special class. The spoken language, being easy to learn, was an all-purpose language. The written language, being in short supply, was for the most part commissioned by those who ruled. They called it into being to give orders; to glorify their deeds whether they were glorious or not; to provide the solace of religion; or all three at once.

The written language was obviously of not much immediate use in the transmission of knowledge or what might be called cultural diffusion, considering in this instance culture as that which makes a society of an agglomeration. It did not reach enough people. That was firmly in the hands of (loosely speaking) the poets and the performers. The poets mastered the arts of rhythm and rhyme and alliteration, all of which simplified the task of memorizing long, arid accounts; the performers turned all the special qualities of the spoken—the performed—language to account in bringing those accounts to the masses. The Homerian epics were first written down thousands of years after their creation; meanwhile, along with the oeuvres of other poets and of dramatists, they served the early Greeks much as the Encyclopaedia Britannica served the English-speaking world, or at least used to before Mortimer Adler got his hands on it. The most effective manner of refreshing oneself on matters of Greek technology was by calling to mind the appropriate passages in the Odyssey.

Then came the next step, and that step was decisive. Again, exactly how it came about is largely a matter of speculation, although by now we have passed the period we call prehistory (that is a tautology, but I shall not apologize), and it is likely that in time a good deal more will be known about it. Since it was a process that occurred over some extensive period of time, there must have been intermediate stages, and it is not difficult to imagine what they may have been. But imagination can go only so far, and the rest is something for the experts.

The enormous step forward was the realization that the kinds of noises made by man at any given time and place for purposes of communication were relatively few in number and that accordingly it would be child's play (literally) to codify them and remember them. It turns out that for virtually all known languages there are forty to fifty such noises, or more accurately, forty or fifty kinds of noises which are recognized as being distinct noises and are part of the language. They are by no means the same in all languages. French and Spanish, for example, recognize two quite different sounds for what the English-speaking world calls *r*. In the part of Mexico where I once lived, there is no clear distinction between the sounds we are accustomed to represent with a *b* and those we represent with a *v*, although both letters are in use. Closer to home, there are parts of the United States in which the three words *Mary, merry,* and *marry* are quite easily distinguishable, and other parts where the pronunciation of all three is very nearly identical.

At this point, I regret to say, things become extremely untidy. Only professional linguists employ an alphabet with forty or fifty letters. Written languages in ordinary use make do with twenty-five or so. They make up the difference in part by the employment of letter combinations, such as *ch* and *sh* in English, or accents or diereses or tildes, or in a variety of other manners.

But untidy or not, the effect of the shift from the pictograph (or the hieroglyphic, which was a degenerate form of the pictograph) to the alphabet was to reduce the spoken language and the written language from two symbol systems to two related forms of the same symbol system. The spoken language so easily learned could be converted to the written language and back with relatively little added effort—little, that is to say, when compared with the effort of learning a wholly different system.

And the consequences were beyond belief. Sometime about 500 B.C., somewhere in the neighborhood of the Mediterranean, this new technology known as "the alphabet" began to come into general use. Now, for the very first time, an ordinary human being could make a durable record of what he knew or what he thought or what he wished to say. He no longer had to invest so enormous an amount of time and effort in simply learning to write that he had neither time nor energy to know anything else, or think anything else, or say anything else. There had been, before then, a well-defined and specialized craft practiced by men known as "scribes"; like goldsmiths and court jesters, they served those in power. The craft remained in a new form, but now it could be practiced by anyone who had the urge and the opportunity (it was not an egalitarian society), and they could serve whom they pleased, including above all themselves.

(This phase of human development is considered in detail and most provocatively in Preface to Plato, by Eric Havelock. I have borrowed from him here.)

I have called the alphabet a "technology," which may be stretching the word a bit farther than I can justify. "Praxis," I imagine, would be more precise, but it is not a common word. In any case, I choose my word because of the significance it carries. We have come to learn that technologies have consequences that are anything but immediately obvious, and some of those consequences are more important than the technology itself, if that makes any sense.

The point that Havelock makes, and that he maintains Plato had in mind when he wrote The Republic, is that the dissemination of writing skills had the effect of stripping the poet and the performer of their roles as custodians of the culture and turning that obligation, or privilege, over to the scholar, the student, and above all the cogitator, the thinker, the reasoner. The talents of the poet and the performer are great, and not to be scorned, but they are directed a good deal more toward the heart than at the head. There is nothing at all wrong with that, but the outcome differs considerably. The poet and the performer, at their best, may lead man to aspire; the thinker, the cogitator, makes it possible to attain.

The glorious achievement of the Greeks—that sudden marvelous burst of intellectual vitality that still underlies much of what we think and believe—was a technological triumph. When a religion came to predominate which strangled that technology, the vitality vanished; it reappeared only when the grip of that religion was loosened. Alphabetic writing made cumulative knowledge possible and generally available, and that is what we live upon today.

It is interesting, in passing, to consider where the Greeks failed, for that, too, is connected with a symbol system. Intoxicated, perhaps, with the alphabet, they chose to employ letters of the alphabet to denominate numbers, and never managed to arrive at the notion of a positional system of notation. As a consequence, even elementary computation was a task for specialists, and the Greeks made virtually no progress in mathematics beyond geometry, which deals not with numbers but with space. (What they did do with numbers tended itself to be geometrical, which is why we speak of "square numbers" and "cube roots" and "conic sections.") The mathematics upon which we now rely did not truly begin to take shape until the sixteenth century or so.

Unfortunately, the process of mapping the spoken language on the written language must be performed under extremely unfavorable circumstances. The written language, being as it is an instrument for use in making records, is designed for stability and reliability. The spoken language, in contrast, is in a constant state of flux, as we are all aware and as I shall be reminding you constantly. Maps of any kind are in trouble when the area being mapped is, for example, a sandy coast in an area buffeted by angry storms and high tides. The spoken language changes; its map does not easily do so.

Thus the pronunciation of the first syllable of the words *either* and *neither* has oscillated over the years among the vowel sound in *pray,* in *preen* and in *pry.* At the moment, "pry" seems to be the favorite, "preen" is a close second, "pray" is pretty much out of the running. What will be the case in fifty years no one can say with any assurance: if someone with a thick Irish accent becomes a television anchorman—which is unlikely—we may all be saying "nayther."

The English language, moreover, is as copious as it is because it has always borrowed freely from other languages. As uninhibited as most borrowers, it generally snatches not only the sound but the spelling. "Nation" is not a particularly well-mapped spelling of the word for a Frenchman, but at least it can be understood as a consequence of the evolution of the language and the nature of human physiology; it makes no sense whatever in English. But we have it, and we live with it. Where such spellings as "enough" and "through" and "freight" come from I do not know, although I imagine that reference to the Oxford English Dictionary might tell me.

(This, I do believe, is the first reference I have made to the Oxford English Dictionary, hereafter to be referred to as the OED. It is the world's only real English dictionary, out of date as it may be; the rest, although useful in various degrees, are really guides to usage and hence express nothing more than opinions. The OED provides a scrupulous history of the written English word and assumes no further authority. Buy one, if you can get up the cash.)

Taking the language as a whole for purposes of special pleading, there is justification for variant spellings of almost any word you may choose. The classic example is "ghoti," with the gh as in "enough," the o as in "women," and the ti as in "nation," all of which spells out "fish." But I could safely spell "language" as "langwidge," or "purposes" as "perposes" or even "perposez," or "word" as "wurd."

This is a matter of great distress for tidy folk, and there is a steady flow of proposals for reform of English spelling. George Bernard Shaw bequeathed his not inconsiderable fortune for the purpose, and when Colonel McCormick owned the *Chicago Tribune* he insisted that the spellings "frate" and "thru" be used, although as far as I know he continued to spell "Colonel" in customary fashion.

The conventional wisdom has been that such proposals fly in the face of the fact that the spoken language changes whether we like it or not, and that the reform would have to be repeated at regular intervals until the end of time, or of English. (And the entire literature of the language be reprinted each time.) I am not any longer certain of that, although I once was; it may be that television and such will freeze the language to a far larger extent than was once possible. Still, I am opposed, just as I am opposed to introduction of the metric system, for I do not see why my world should be reorganized to make things easier for children, and backward children at that.

Having made my way once, at least, around Robin Hood's barn, I can resume the search for lucidity that remains my principal concern. Spelling is an annoyance, and in the English language certainly more of an annoyance than it absolutely need be. But for the writer, correct spelling is an obligation, and there is no way out.

That is something more than a passion for correctness, or the counsel of pedantry. The person who misspells has made his own mapping of the spoken language on the written language, and assuming that he knows the spoken language, it is likely to be a perfectly respectable mapping in its own right. If a restaurant menu should carry the information that its special offering of the day is "fisch," no one who reads the menu is likely to be confused even for so much as a moment, since he would be disposed to pronounce that word to himself, as he read it, precisely as he would pronounce "fish." And indeed, in that setting and at that level no noticeable damage has been done.

Even in the restaurant, however, the misspelling is a distraction. For a moment or so, the patron's attention has shifted from the consideration of lunch to the consideration of spelling, which is not, after all, what brought him into the restaurant. He recovers quickly enough, and redirects himself to the business at hand. But there was a break in his stride, however momentary.

Reading is difficult, under the best of circumstances. It requires a significant mental effort to reassemble in one's own mind, out of another's vocabulary and syntax and sentence structure and the larger structure of his offering as a whole, precisely what was in his mind when he wrote. He has described something, and your task is to envisage exactly what he is describing; or he has put forward an argument and your task is to follow it closely. A small hiccup in your thought processes may appear inconsequential, but it is really more than you can tolerate.

(In the restaurant, there may also be a passing suspicion that a restaurateur who doesn't know how to spell "fish" probably doesn't know how to cook it. But this is ad hominem, and beneath us. Still . . .)

No one ever really masters spelling in the English language; the evolution of the language has made it far too difficult. I count myself better than most, and considering the sheer number of words I have been called upon to spell in my time, I should be. But a bit back I used the word "dieresis," and agonized over it before I had it right. It happens that the word is spelled exactly as one should expect, but that is not as helpful as it ought to be, since so many words are not.

There is nothing for it but to learn how to spell, which is achieved by worrying about spelling, and by reading a great deal. The writer must concern himself with spelling, every moment of the way. Flaubert exerted himself to find the *mot juste,* and a laudable exertion it was, but a misspelled word can never be *juste.* If I absolutely had to make the choice—which patently I do not— I would far rather write "light purple" than misspell "mauve."

There is, however, a pedagogical problem involved. The child first learning to write is embarking upon the first truly difficult task of his life, and it will be a great many years before he encounters another even nearly as difficult. At that stage there are more important things than spelling to exercise his mind, and there are those knowledgeable in the ambiance of the second grade who propose to defer a concern with spelling to another time. I am not qualified to rule on such matters, but I am persuaded that at some point the child must be told that he cannot spell improperly and hope to become President, churchwarden, or third baseman of the New York Yankees. All those statements are gross falsehoods, but lying to children has never seemed to me to be a heinous crime and I hold it to be now and then absolutely essential. And it is true that if the child never gains respect for spelling, he will not ever become a competent expository writer, for no craftsman can be competent who does not respect his tools.

As I proceed, I expect to be writing a great deal about the computer, although it may not be clear right now what the computer has to do with the written word. The analogies between the computer and the human brain are richly informative, as long as it is recognized that the fundamental purpose of analogy is to reveal differences and not similarities. The computer deals with a written language of its own, but it is a written language that does not have a spoken language as its referent. Consequently, the computer cannot tolerate misspellings. It may very well be that a child who learns to read and write with the aid of a computer will have a quite different attitude toward spelling, and will learn it with smaller protest.

But it will still be hard.

Chapter Five

A Word or Two

> "But 'glory' doesn't mean 'a nice knockdown argument,'" Alice objected.
>
> "When *I* use a word," Humpty Dumpty said, in rather a scornful tone, "it means just what I choose it to mean—neither more nor less."
>
> LEWIS CARROLL, Through the Looking-Glass

I HAVE perhaps been frivolous in devoting so much of our time to the alphabet for no better reason than my own antiquary zeal, and to no better end than to make the obvious point that writers should be able to spell or if they have the necessary resources should find someone or something to spell for them. Spelling is simply part of the tedious mechanics of writing, and a kind of no-win enterprise, since the writer gains no real ground by spelling correctly but loses ground if he cannot manage it.

Moving up the next step in complexity, to the word, is another matter altogether. It, too, is a symbol, but where the letter is symbol for a sound, the word is symbol for some kind of observation or experience: the name we assign, by social compact, to a more or less unitary interaction between our own central nervous systems and something else. I am obliged to be that vague, for I must not let myself forget that the word has not the sharp edges that my description seems to imply, and that one of the most

49

common uses of the word is to describe the interaction of the central nervous system with itself or with another word.

As I noted earlier, it is not quite as easy as one might expect to be certain just what a word is. I noted, too, that the computer sometimes brings a kind of clarity to these matters that the natural language does not possess. If you choose to write, as I do, on a word processor, you will be struck by the fact that the computer deals with two quite different kinds of word, each carefully defined. (Everything about a computer is carefully defined.) One kind of word is a set of characters of almost any sort which is both preceded and followed by a blank space. As far as the computer is concerned, such a word does not have to mean anything at all; it is a typographical arrangement and that is the end of it. The other kind of word is any one of the very limited, wholly arbitrary sets of characters that the computer has been constructed or instructed to recognize and respond to. At some levels it is essential that such computer words, too, be bracketed by blank spaces; at others it is not.

If the natural language is approached analytically, the arbitrary nature of the *word,* as the computer recognizes it, is well kept in mind. From that point of view, a word of itself does not necessarily carry meaning: to do so it must be interpreted in association with other words. Indeed, the practice of analyzing single words, or small groups of words, may lead to something close to madness.

I am not for a moment deprecating the practice of analyzing single words, for in its place it possesses its own interest and I, for one, find it fascinating. In one of its aspects, exhaustively represented by the OED, it deals with the history of a word's usage as it has passed down the centuries within a single language and as it has passed from language to language. Such analysis is of some practical use to the expository writer, but in a very limited way, and I shall defer its consideration for the moment. It is of far more practical use to the psychologist, for it tells him much of the interaction between people and their spoken language. Thus, there is a certain insight to be gained by the awareness that many or most words in common use to denote sexual intercourse stem from earlier usages that denoted violence. (Or from present usages: note the slang word *bang*.)

But at some point, the analysis of usage becomes pedanticism. To employ a word, or shun it, with an undue reverence for the meaning that it once possessed or that it possesses in other languages is to act the fool. Where the spoken language is concerned, meaning derives almost altogether from current usage. Where the written language is concerned, it will usually derive from recent usage, and current usage does not provide trustworthy guidance. But the written language changes more slowly than the spoken language, although every bit as inexorably.

Let me try to make this clear by an example, which I can draw from the very subject under consideration. I would naturally write in a book of this sort that the quality of a writer's diction has a significant effect upon the quality of his prose. Yet I would never dream of using the word *diction* to mean "the choice of words" in ordinary conversation. That is precisely what *diction* meant until a relatively few years ago, and indeed the OED carries only that definition and other closely related definitions going back to the sixteenth century, when *diction* meant "word" and nothing more. But *diction* is now a word employed in evaluating competing television announcers, few of whom themselves choose any of the words they use, but have their words chosen for them by people like me and even, from time to time, by me. In any case, it makes no difference in the long run; "choice of words" says exactly what "diction" used to say, and is neither better nor worse than "diction" for the purpose. This will not satisfy the pedants, of course, which is why we call them pedants.

We can pass rapidly over the other kind of analysis of the individual word, since it has little or no bearing on the subject at hand. Words also change over time for physiological reasons having to do with the manner in which our vocal system makes noises. I wrote earlier of the word *nation* and said the French pronounce that word more or less as it is spelled. In fact, the French pronounce the *ion* as it is spelled, but pronounce the *t* as a soft *c*. The combination *tio* exists in Latin, precursor of French, and although no one at all now knows how the Romans pronounced their language, it is generally assumed that it was pronounced as it was spelled. The Gauls simply took the easy way out: it required more energy than it was worth to articulate the letters *t, i* and *o* in succession. Changes of that sort, driven by what might be called efficiency, take place all the time, particularly within words which are often used. They are not always reflected in spelling, and we continue to write "Wednesday," but we no longer say "Wednesday." Sometimes the spelling comes to conform, as when "Newtown" becomes "Newton," and the like. But all that is by the by.

Returning to etymology, as I promised I would: it cannot be entirely ignored. Meanings once associated with a word do not necessarily die outright; they continue to twitch feebly from time to time, and perhaps a good deal more than feebly when they are permitted to invade a metaphor. One might be tempted to write "He collapsed in a quivering mass, on tenterhooks lest he be recognized." But "tenterhooks" etymologically signifies an apparatus upon which fabrics are stretched taut, and the metaphor suddenly becomes grotesque. The risk in this instance is slight, but present, and a scrupulous writer will always worry about such slip-ups. This is a counsel of excellence, for the most scrupulous writer in the world will fall into a trap from time to time. "Scrupulous," by the way, comes from a Latin word meaning "pebble." Would it be permissible to write, say, "enormously scrupulous"?

The word, in any case, is the building block of the written as of the spoken language. Whatever might appear to be the case to an illiterate visitor from another planet, the act of writing is the act of setting down one word after another and not, as it might appear, the act of setting down one letter after another. When I am obliged to decide between two words more or less similar in meaning, it will generally make a difference where my choice falls; when I am obliged to choose between two spellings, both correct, as in the instance of "judgment" and "judgement," it makes no difference at all unless my reader has been persuaded by a grammar-school teacher that one or the other is "correct." (And even then it makes no practical difference, since there is no way I can possibly tell which of the two spellings captured her fancy and thus became a part of the reader's own cultural heritage.)

The writer, then, calls upon his own vocabulary. If he is created like all the rest of us, he possesses three distinct vocabularies at least, and in all likelihood the hazy outlines of two others. Only two of the five are likely to be available to him as he writes, and only one is generally useful, but he should be aware of them all.

Each of us possesses a passive vocabulary that is positively enormous. It is defined by the words we understand, or very nearly understand, or believe we understand, when we read them or hear them. (I should take account, I suppose, of the practical fact that at the margins we may be familiar with a written word but not be able to recognize it when it is spoken, or vice versa. It is not a matter of very much importance.) That vocabulary comes into being by what we hear and what we read; in the first instance it is created by the cultural environment, or environments, in which we each of us make our lives; in the second instance largely by the opportunities that we make or seize, or that are thrust upon us.

The second vocabulary is the active vocabulary, and comprises the words we can call upon when we speak or write. For most of us the active vocabulary is smaller than the passive by at least a factor of ten—it would not be difficult in principle to make estimates for various subjects and I suppose it has been done. In view of the preposterously large number of distinct words in the English language, to which it is reasonable for us to limit ourselves for the moment, the active vocabulary of the average American is tiny: a few thousand words at most. I seem to recall from earlier days that as judged from literary output, Shakespeare possessed the largest recorded active vocabulary and that it came to approximately twenty thousand words. We do not have an absolute need for any great number of words. As I can testify, if one wishes to get along quite comfortably in a foreign language, an active vocabulary of no more than a few hundred words is adequate. I have noticed that in foreign languages the disparity between my own active and passive vocabularies is tremendous, but I do not know whether that is unusual—I suspect it is not—or what it signifies.

The remaining vocabularies are a good deal more amorphous, and in two instances idiosyncratic as well. One is constituted of a number of words, by no means negligibly small, which are to be found in any individual's vocabulary as distinct assemblages of sounds, or letters, but which for some reason or another—and I cannot guess what the reason may be—have no place in either the active or the passive vocabulary. In time and with effort, they can usually be mastered. I can identify a few for myself out of hand. *Rebarbative* was once such a word for me, but I now own it. *Subfusc* is still such a word, and all the reading of C. P. Snow, who had a strange passion for *subfusc,* doesn't help; I must still look it up each time I see it.

There is also what might be called a candidate vocabulary, consisting of words looking for entry into one of the earlier three. These are words newly acquired and being tested for general utility, and they are likely to be overused, just as possession of a new crosscut saw will tempt its owner into sawing everything in sight, whether it needs it or not. No lasting damage is done: sooner or later the word will either enter one of the other vocabularies or it will not, and in the meantime a certain amount of discipline will assure that most of its intrusions will be excised in the second draft, which is more than can be achieved with a crosscut saw.

Finally, there is the specialist vocabulary. Most of us have one, and parts of others. I myself, as the consequence of a misspent youth, am or was some kind of expert at contract bridge, and I continue to possess the specialist vocabulary that goes with that state. I employ, readily and without conscious thought, such words as *Deschapelles* and *tenace* and *Drury,* which in all likelihood have no meaning to you at all, as well as such words as *strip* and *punch* and *uppercut,* none of which mean what you might expect.

This vocabulary exists only in a corner of my mind, from which I extract it when necessary and only when necessary. It is, at those moments, extremely useful and extremely precise.

As among individuals, no two of those active vocabularies, or passive vocabularies, or defective vocabularies, or candidate vocabularies, or specialist vocabularies, are exactly alike at even the superficial level, although the specialist vocabulary comes close. I know words you don't know, and you know words I don't know, no matter what it is we mean when we say "know." (At a deeper level, as I have said earlier, we are likely to mean significantly different things by words we do have in common, but I am not at that level now.) Considering the English-speaking population as a whole, there is a good deal of overlap, and discourse of any kind is carried on preponderantly within the area of that universal overlap: all the bread-and-butter conversation and run-of-the-mill writing. We really have very little trouble understanding each other as we go about our humdrum affairs.

The expository writer, however, is not at the humdrum level. He is writing, presumably, because he has something uncommon to communicate, or thinks he has. He cannot rely on that area of universal overlap; he is not likely to be able to say uncommon things in that common a language. The expository writer must care about words, for his tool is language, and the most important language we possess begins with words.

You will notice that there is an important asymmetry between the writer and the reader. The writer has only his active vocabulary to call upon; the candidate vocabulary is for the time being more a nuisance than anything else. The reader, on the other hand, is employing his passive vocabulary, which is far more copious. In the absence of such a mismatch, the task of communication would be close to impossible, for beyond words in common use, which are the small change of a good working vocabulary, the overlap among active vocabularies is not nearly as large as one would like to have it.

The writer is also well served by the redundancy of the language, and indeed a practiced writer will exploit it. To say something twice is prudent, makes it less likely that communication will proceed at a pace that is wearying to the reader, and in a way is courteous so long as it is not overdone. Over time, the language itself has been structured for redundancy, as those of us who once transmitted long narratives by way of Western Union had good reason to know. As a consequence, the meaning of words that have never before been encountered by the reader will often be quite satisfactorily revealed by the context. Indeed, this is the manner in which any given vocabulary expands. We rarely go to the dictionary or the thesaurus, except to sharpen our acquaintance with a word with which we are already more or less familiar.

These are comforts for the writer, but they do not relieve him of his responsibilities. He is still obliged to exert his best efforts to maximize the overlap between his own vocabulary, as it appears in whatever it is he is writing, and the passive vocabulary of those who are to read it. I shall qualify that assertion a bit as I proceed, but not so much as to diminish its importance.

Only now can I strip some of the dissimulation from my earlier consideration of lucidity. Lucidity is not an absolute, at least in the natural language, but a relation between those who are engaged in the act of communication, which in the context of these pages is writing and reading. Since it is the writer who initiates the act and is pretty much in control of it, it is the writer who is responsible for the health of the relation. He exercises that responsibility by carrying throughout the writing process a keen awareness of the nature of the audience for which he writes. One of his obligations is to tailor his vocabulary, among all the other aspects of his writing, to that audience, as part of the process of achieving the lucidity which is his goal.

Under certain circumstances, considerations of that sort govern the choice of words. Where a precise word is available that the writer knows to be in the armory of his readers, he may not use a word that is less precise, for it will irritate where it does not confuse. Thus, over the range of ordinary discourse, the words *number* and *numeral* are as good as synonymous and may be so employed. Even over much of the range of mathematical discourse they are synonymous. But in the latter instance, there are occasions upon which they are not, and on those occasions it is the obligation of the writer writing for mathematicians to know the distinction and to honor it.

It is just that obligation that makes certain forms of writing incomprehensible to all but those who are within some sort of inner circle of their own. There is writing that maximizes lucidity for a relative few at the price of opacity for all the rest. It is not a lamentable practice; it is necessary and useful, as long as the writer is fully aware of what he is doing. It is only when the writer writes for an audience in a language inappropriate for that audience that any kind of crime is being committed. Unfortunately, it is a common crime. It is understandable, and perhaps even forgivable, when the lawyer, say, is trying to write for a general audience. It is unforgivable when a man whose craft is writing directs his words to an audience of lawyers without taking care that his choice of words maximizes lucidity in those circumstances.

It is essential that the writer define his audience and have it in the forefront of his mind at every stage of his writing. That definition will be as precise as he can make it, which is all that can be expected of him. It governs his choice of words, which is what we are discussing here, and a great deal else, which we will get to.

This book is directed to what I am accustomed to call "an intelligent lay audience." Since it is about writing, I may reasonably assume that it is to be read, if at all, by those interested in writing, who will also be those interested in reading, and who will accordingly have a quite copious passive vocabulary. Some will have a specialist vocabulary, but that vocabulary is no concern of mine at the moment. It is conceivable also that some of them will have a specialist vocabulary designed for exactly the matters with which this book is concerned, and may very well have already thrown this book aside because I went through all kinds of contortions, and even was guilty of some imprecision, for no better reason than what they infer to be an inability to use the word *phoneme*. My withers are unwrung.

Phoneme is a technical word employed by linguists to signify sounds which are functionally identical within a given language although they may in fact be readily recognized as quite different sounds. Thus, it rarely makes any difference how hard a speaker makes the pronunciation of *ch* in such a word as *change;* if he should say something that might better be spelled "shange" he will still be understood. If he said "kange" he would not. As a practical matter, few of the sounds made by a foreigner speaking English are identical with the sounds a native speaker would make, and he need only be careful that they are the same phonemes.

I can and do use the word *phoneme,* but not here, because it does not maximize lucidity for the audience I am addressing. I used the sentence *"My withers are unwrung"* because it may very well serve the ends of lucidity for the audience I *do* have in mind (I have not got to sentences yet, but when I do I shall say why) even though it may be no more than a mystery, and consequently an irritant, to my friends the linguists.

It will come as no surprise—indeed, I have said as much already —that the writer is engaged in the search for the *mot juste* as an essential aspect of his struggle to achieve lucidity. It would be a solace if that could be accomplished no more laboriously than by making one's way to the nearest supermarket where the resident bookstore will provide a copy of Roget's Thesaurus, or alternatively to one's supplier of word-processing software so that one may load the same vademecum into one's computer. Roget, however, is neither necessary nor sufficient. I am quite prepared to argue that the writer who employs Roget is not a writer at all, although he may be sincerely employed in trying to become one.

Exactly what it is that makes one *mot* more *juste* than another is a matter with which we have already dealt. Quite obviously, it is the word that carries the burden of meaning the writer intends it to carry, and does so most efficiently and least ambiguously. But as I have been at pains to assert, efficiency and lucidity lie in the relation between writer and reader, and cannot be entirely managed without consideration of that relationship. Whatever the dictionary may say is the meaning of *vademecum,* the word means nothing at all to a person unfamiliar with it and lacking the presumed benefits of an education in Latin, unless that meaning has been carried by the context.

Then, too, there is the matter of tone to be considered. Every word that is expected to perform more than the drudgery of grammatical machinery exists in some kind of cloud of connotations, most of them arising out of the fashion in which that word has been previously used or in which it is currently used. Referring to Roget above, I chose the word *vademecum* with cold-blooded intent. I could have used *reference book,* which carries a minimum of connotation. I could have used *companion* or a word of that general sort; it would have intimated warmth and support. I used *vademecum* because it has become a word that sneers slightly, and I intended a slight sneer.

I seem to have carried this assault on Roget to the point where I am obliged to be more explicit about it. To use a word that is not in the writer's own active vocabulary is a dangerous tactic. It is an unfamiliar tool, and you are likely to cut yourself: to miss its connotations, mistake its tone, handle it clumsily. To be sure, such a word will in almost all instances be in the writer's passive vocabulary, but that is not quite enough. The words he is accustomed to use are brothers; this one is no more than a second cousin, and we all know about second cousins. To use a word that is in neither the active nor the passive vocabulary is sheer folly.

Indeed, the practiced writer is far more likely to use a word and then look it up than to travel the other way around. Each of us can identify, in the outlying areas of his active vocabulary, words he may hesitate to use because he is not entirely certain exactly what they mean. Oddly enough, in such instances he will often be well aware of the connotations they carry, and the connotations may be exactly what he has in mind. Writing along as I am doing now, he will barefacedly use the word, with a mental note to look it up later.

Flaubert, master of the *mot juste,* is supposed to have suspended writing for days on end while he concentrated his attention upon determining exactly, precisely, indubitably and inescapably just what the next word should be. That may or may not be any more than fable. I do not believe it myself, but I did not know Flaubert. If indeed he wrote in that fashion, he was very much alone among those who pass any large part of their time setting words on paper.

As a matter of practical fact, almost all the words a writer puts down are quite as *juste* as Flaubert at his most niggling would want them to be. A few are not, and the author quite often will recognize that to be so. Indeed, he may even be aware that a far better word exists in his active vocabulary but is in hiding for the moment: a perfect word, a lapidary word, a word without fault or flaw. (I shall look up *lapidary* later.) If he is at all practiced at his craft, he will thereupon perform an extremely rapid search of his vocabulary. If a better word comes to him, in it will go. If after a second or two, and not ever very much more, the word does not come, he simply leaves matters where they stand and presses ahead with his writing. And I would gamble that Flaubert did the same, whatever he may have told his friends at the local bistro.

To do otherwise is simply a waste of time. Searching the memory, whatever the purpose, unless immediately successful carries one sooner or later into a maze, pursuing an endless series of false trails and usually wandering farther and farther from one's goals. That process must be ruthlessly broken, so that the false trails may be forgotten and the search begun fresh at a later time, when it may very well be instantaneously successful. Under most circumstances—as when looking for a book you are certain you put down somewhere—it is almost impossible to bring yourself to break off the search. When you are writing it is easy, for you are doing a specific job and the job is what you really want to get on with, not the search for a word.

Dealing with words, we are still at the lowest level of writing. (The alphabet really doesn't have much to do with it at all.) But even at this level, we are beginning to impinge upon the fundamental fact about the craft: it is not an act but a process. It is a process, moreover, which in any given undertaking never finishes. It is terminated at some point or another, because it must be; not because it is finished, but because for one reason or another it is not worth continuing.

Since most expository writing is produced with some kind of explicit purpose, there is a point at which it may be said to be complete, just as a road may be said to be complete when, as planned, it begins in New York and ends in Los Angeles. But the exact form the road may take is infinitely variable, and it is reasonable to postulate that one of those forms may be better for the purpose than any other. It is doubtful that any road has ever actually been constructed that can be said to be in the best possible form, and I am convinced that the equivalent is true of everything that has ever been written, although at times when I read Shakespeare I waver.

The writer must be prepared to proceed through a series of drafts until, for sufficient reasons, he desists. At one extreme, writing a casual letter, he will desist after the first draft. At the other extreme, found most commonly among poets, where the relative brevity of the task makes it less forbidding, and among the producers of textbooks for use in higher education, the redrafting continues until senility or after. Writing is an act performed by human beings, and as a general rule the redrafting ends at death, but survivors have been known to continue it.

A bit more remains to be said about the *mot juste*. It will be, at times, a jarring word, and jarring by design. When a word is chosen so, the purpose is in large part to break a monotony of a presentation or, to put the matter somewhat more crudely, to allay the deadening effect of a presentation that is always at the same level. Judicious doses of incongruity, as long as they are inoffensive and not too outrageous, add to the general tone of the writing. What is generally called "lively writing" is more often than not writing laced with the unexpected.

Earlier I spoke of misspelling as being not so much a sin in itself but a distraction, which in terms of the purposes of expository writing may be equated with sin. Incongruity is certainly a distraction; it is intended to be. But unlike misspelling, it does not offend by marring. It is a constructive distraction, which at its best adds to the sharpness of the writing. It does no violence to what the writer is about, but reinforces it in a somewhat different fashion.

This is patently a self-indulgent book, and I shall reminisce. In my earlier years I enjoyed a passing acquaintance with a colleague who had mastered the art of interpolated incongruity. Joe Palmer had been professor of English at the University of Kentucky, but a fondness for hard liquor and raffish acquaintances, joined in his case with considerable affection for horse racing, brought him unerringly to journalism and in the end to the *New York Herald Tribune,* where he and Red Smith were the two best sports columnists this world has ever known. In one of his columns, Joe reported one morning the details of converting alcoholic beverages into a form of jelly. That technological advance, Joe wrote in his own elegant prose, created a whole new freedom for a sensitive lady riding on a train, "since if she were just eating jelly on her biscuit nobody would pay any particular attention, and she could be stiff as a mink by Philadelphia."

But Joe Palmer has carried me far beyond the mere matter of words, and into broader concerns, although it may not be immediately noticeable. I have not finished with the subject, for there is much more to be said about words and I shall no doubt find the opportunity to say at least some of it. For the moment, however, we shall pass along to other matters.

Chapter Six

Man's Best Friend

Neither the naked hand nor the understanding
left to itself can effect much. It is by
instruments and helps that the work is done,
which are as much wanted for the
understanding as for the hand.

FRANCIS BACON, Novum Organum

I HAVE ALLUDED from time to time in the preceding pages to the computer or the word processor (the two are not quite the same kinds of object) and I suspect I shall be alluding to it more and more as we proceed. Let me now depart from my orderly sequence and consider the word processor briefly in its own right.

As even the least among us is by now aware, the word processor is an electronic device intended to be used in the act of writing. In one form, it is a fairly elaborate device which is designed for that purpose and no other and which can perform typographical miracles, filling the page with all sorts of gaudy wiggles and wags and effusions of the spirit and accordingly dear to the heart of the adman and the direct-mail impresario, among others. In that form, it is generally known as a business word processor or a dedicated word processor, as you may choose.

I shall call it in its other form the *personal word processor*, although I do not recall that any such phrase is generally used. In that form, it is a language that can be loaded into a personal computer. The personal word processor can produce a few of the wags and wiggles of its relative, but not all of them, and it does so with some difficulty. The assemblage as a whole, however, can also behave most efficiently as a computer, which the dedicated word processor cannot. Neither, of course, has either the computing power or the potential word-processing power of the monstrous IBM machines. But they are a good deal cheaper: the dedicated word processor can be had for a few thousand dollars and the personal word processor for not many hundreds. The electronic typewriter at the moment lies in between and will probably disappear sooner or later, since there is no good reason for having one; it is neither a first-rate word processor nor any serious kind of computer, and exists only because secretaries over thirty and other such worthies are terrified of anything that bears the scent of computery and not anxious to displace the tricks they know for new ones.

Now that the distinctions have been made, I shall speak of the personal word processor simply as the *word processor,* since we will not be dealing here with any of the other members of the family. I was merely trying to set the record straight.

Personal word processors, and indeed word processors in general, have not been with us for long, and it would be well to take a closer look at them before we all begin to take them for granted. Bear with me; I intend to go back to the roots, which I shall find in the typewriter.

That familiar device is a machine which makes marks on paper. The marks are for the most part letters and associated symbols; the marks themselves are made by ink. If I may be permitted a locution, the typewriter paints a message on a sheet of paper, and then another on another sheet of paper, and continues to do so until the message or the paper or the paint gives out. And that is exactly what a word processor does, finally.

The difficulty with the typewriter is that what it does it does so well. The paper is durable, and the ink sticks to it, or rather in it.

Those are necessary characteristics, for the typewriter would not be worth much if they were not present. Here, too, the word processor does no less.

If for any reason that you may assign the typewriter paints a message which is wrong in any respect, there is the devil to pay. Let us say that the typist tapped out: "This is the eighth time it happened," and later decided, or discovered, that the proper message was: "This is the fourth time it happened." Changing "eighth" to "fourth" takes time and labor. In the old days it meant rubbing the paper furiously with an eraser, always an untidy process, and then typing the new word in. The glories of technology have since provided somewhat simpler methods, but they are less than perfect. And in any case, they do not work if the right word was "fifth," which would leave a space, or worse still "eleventh," which could not be fitted in.

It gets even worse. Perhaps it was, after all, the hundred and thirtieth time it had happened. That could not possibly be shrunk to fit the space formerly occupied by "eighth." Indeed, if such a change had to be made in the third paragraph of a forty-page document, it could be done neatly only by retyping the entire document, more often than not. The alternative would be an untidy document, or if ten or twelve such changes had to be made, an extremely untidy document. There are very good reasons not to want an extremely untidy document, and we shall be dealing with some of them as we go along.

And all these have been trivial changes. There are less trivial changes to be contemplated as well: changing the order of words in a sentence, or sentences in a paragraph. All together, they made typing wearisome and costly. I say this with regret; I loved my typewriter. But facts must be faced.

Then came that familiar miracle the cathode-ray tube, better known as the television screen. Like the typewriter, it paints messages. The painting is far more complex than anything the typewriter can manage, but for the moment that is beside the point. It does not paint with ink and paper but with points of light on a sheet of coated glass, in a fashion we need not understand. And those points of light can be turned on and off at will, leaving no trace of any noticeable kind. Indeed, an ordinary television screen can and does paint an entirely new message thirty times a second, hour after hour, without any kind of fuss at all. If you absolutely had to have it faster, it would be no problem.

The word processor interposes that screen between the keyboard—an ordinary typewriter keyboard—upon which the message is composed and the paper—ordinary paper—upon which it is to be printed. The paper need not be printed until the message has been properly composed on the screen. Everything else the word processor does—and there is a great deal more—follows from that.

The computer tells those lights when to go on and off (among other things). In its memory the computer houses instructions that can be carried out in thousandths of a second by messages from the keyboard; those instructions are placed in its memory by a word-processing program. There are dozens of such programs. The writer buys the program of his choice, learns the code by means of which communication is established, and goes about his business.

I am using such a program at this moment, and I know the code. Indeed, I used it just before I began this paragraph: The code in question advised me to place ".a" at a certain place on the screen, and the instructions advised the computer that the code was not part of my message, and was not to be subsequently printed. I am now about to place another code—".b"—at another point on the screen, and ".in 20" at still a third point, after which I shall type a few more codes on the keyboard, quite as simple, with which I shall not trouble you.

> I am using such a program at this moment, and I know the code. Indeed, I used it just before I began this paragraph: The code in question advised me to place ".a" at a certain place on the screen, and the instruc-

tions advised the computer that the code was not part
of my message, and was not to be subsequently printed.
I am now about to place another code—".b"—at another point on the screen, and ".in 20" at still a third
point, after which I shall type a few more codes on the
keyboard, quite as simple, with which I shall not trouble
you.

And see what happened!

What the computer did, at my command, was copy the paragraph I had just written, insert it into the text, and indent it twenty
spaces. I must admit that I have never before done such a thing
and cannot imagine the circumstances, other than this very special circumstance, when I would want to. I chose to do it here
because the result is so obvious, and that it is also trivial need not
bother us. Entering the various commands added perhaps two
seconds to my typing time, and executing them took the word
processor perhaps another two seconds.

In all the senses that have any meaning, the word processor will
cheerfully do what I tell it to do. I did not originally write the
sentence you just read; what I wrote was ". . . do exactly what I
tell it to do." But I then decided that the word "exactly" was
superfluous, and a half second later it was gone, leaving no trace
behind. Any one of a dozen word-processing programs would do
the same, quite as cheerfully.

To sum it up, the word processor is a device that will paint upon
a cathode-ray tube several hundred different pages—different, at
times, in only a single character—in the time it takes a stenogra-
pher to paint one page on paper. The labor involved in editing
those pages, aside from the labor of composing them, is also done
by the computer; when I finally decide that the page is exactly as
I wish it to be, the computer orders it printed, and stores an
electronic version for my files. My typewriter gathers dust; I cannot imagine using it again.

The computer is generally regarded as a number-cruncher, and
it does crunch numbers with great abandon, if asked to do so. But

it is more sensible to think of it as a machine that manipulates symbols as more familiar machine tools manipulate matter, and since language itself is a symbol system, just as numbers are, the computer is quite capable of handling language when instructed to do so. The instruction code must be learned, which appears at first glance to be beyond any likelihood of achievement, but in fact all it amounts to is a small, and scarcely noticeable, increment to the codes you have already mastered without any fuss at all, including that particular code known as the elements of the English language.

If you look upon the writer as engaged in arranging letters, or words, or any other such aggregations, the word processor will do that arranging more efficiently and with less fuss than any other method you might imagine. Best of all, unlike certain human word processors, it will not try to make up your mind for you.

It may not be immediately apparent that to make the most efficient use of the word processor a printer of some kind must be attached; it must be attached sooner or later in any case, but not necessarily while the act of composition is being performed. So far as I know, journalists using dedicated word processors do not have access to immediate hard copy (forgive the jargon, but it is self-explanatory in this context) and I suspect they lose from it. But it is a virtue within journalism to write hurriedly, and perhaps the price is worth paying.

A writer of any kind who does not work on a word processor is either dead broke or some kind of fool: it is as simple as that and we should not shilly-shally about it. He may be at the same time an absolutely first-rate writer, but although he may well dispute it, he gains nothing by his abnegation, and only makes life harder for himself and, to a limited extent, for others. At the moment this is nothing more than an unsupported statement, for which I will provide support in a chapter or two.

There are a good many who have not made the move, and who probably never will, among them a horde of my betters. No matter. When I myself first became a journalist, I found myself with a colleague, some fifty years older than I, who viewed the type-writer as Moloch incarnate and did all his writing with pen on paper. (He did, however, use a fountain pen—a great big orange fountain pen.) He was a splendid fellow, and a first-rate journalist. I suspect that there are more than a few creative writers who maintain the same attitude as he did toward the typewriter, let alone the word processor. Bless them all, and let us go about our business.

The larger part of the reluctance stems from the fear that when the machine enters fully into the process of writing it will inevitably change the nature of writing and not merely the brute process itself. That judgment is accurate: it will. But not very much, any more than the typewriter or the steel pen changed it very much. And what change does occur, I suspect, will be for the better. In any case, that kind of change need not be feared. Language and its manipulation are rooted deep within us; they are tough and they are central to our very survival; they are bigger and more powerful than any of the machines they help us build.

Since it may not be immediately apparent what the word processor brings to the process of writing, let me spell out the heart of that process in some detail. As I asserted a few pages back, any writing beyond the level of complexity involved in lettering a road sign is a process of successive approximation. It is most unlikely to meet the need, whatever the need may be, first time around. Writing is a bit like extracting the square root of 2; it gets better with each successive approximation until finally it is as good as it needs to be.

It is all as tedious as anything I know. Not the process of approximation itself: that is a form of writing, which is an activity of the mind and a fascinating activity. It is the machinery of the process that is tedious: the physical acts that accompany writing and editing and reproducing and reediting and rereproducing and on and on. The physical acts associated with writing, I repeat. They are drudgery, and there is nothing redeeming about them. Writing is nothing but enjoyment when it is done in the head. Putting it down, over and over, until it is the way your head vaguely—very vaguely—envisaged it, is quite something else again.

What is more, real writing, as distinct from its machinery, requires concentration. It is most difficult to work with messy material. A page that has been scribbled upon cannot be read with any efficiency so that the new version can be judged against the old; it must first be restored to perfect new copy if the mind is to grasp it whole and set to work revising it once again. Indeed, as a practical matter, a page that has once been scribbled upon cannot even be scribbled upon again; it must be reproduced clean and only then can the scribbling recommence.

The word processor cannot remove all the tedium, but it goes a long way. It is untiring, grinding out the consequences of each approximation clean and neat and tidy, ready to be brutalized once more. No scribbling between the lines, no arrows to indicate what goes where, no striking out of unwanted words or phrases or sentences, no scissors and paste. It is the difference between driving to Philadelphia and crawling there on one's hands and knees. One arrives at Philadelphia in either case, but if crawling were the only way, very few would try, fewer still would succeed, and almost no one would enjoy the trip. They might not enjoy Philadelphia, either, but that is not the present issue.

If this were all the word processor contributed to the writer's well-being, I should think it enough and beyond. But there is more, and I shall try to express it as the occasion arises.

There is also more from a quite different perspective, dealing now not with writing itself but with understanding writing and language itself. Dealing with a word processor, you are engaged in a kind of language and a kind of communication that differ from any with which man has previously been familiar. The language of the word processor itself is arbitrary, precise and extremely limited—far more manageable, in short, than any natural language and infinitely more transparent. Working in it, one is led to consider the question of understanding in the abstract: What is it, and how is it achieved? What are the steps that reduce or eliminate misunderstanding? It can do a writer no harm to give thought to such matters. He may learn.

Obviously, there are questions about dealing with the computer's language and the computer's understanding that parallel questions about our own language and consequently our own understanding. The very bleakness of the computer's world lays the questions bare, and provides a certain kind of clarity in dealing with them in terms of ordinary language and ordinary communication. Those are the questions that haunt the writer and with which he must deal as part of his craft. You have seen some of these considerations in earlier pages, and you will see more as I proceed.

A part of the illumination that emerges out of the use of the word processor is already represented here, and for the moment may even irritate you. At the typewriter, there are devices which are not often employed in ordinary writing, although they are perhaps overemployed in some uses of the written word, such as those of the adman. One avoids them when typing, largely because they are physically distracting.

Some are conventional and nothing more, having nothing to do with the written word itself. Thus, the newspaper for which I once had the honor to work can be variously denominated the "New York Herald Tribune," the New York Herald Tribune, or the New York *Herald Tribune,* as the spirit may move you. My own view, for which I am not prepared to hang, is that the second of these is best, the third is acceptable, the first is least desirable. At the typewriter, however, it is the first that I always employ, since it involves no backspacing and thus less energy and less distraction than the second. The third cannot be accomplished at all. This is of no great consequence; they all say the same thing.

You may have noticed by now that I make free use of underlining and italicization within the text itself. I use the first primarily to indicate the cadence with which a sentence should be read. Your mind will silently read "I don't know how he does it" in a fashion quite different from that in which it reads "I don't know

<u>how</u> he does it," for that interpretation of the underline is as much a part of the language as the meaning assigned to the word *how* itself.

In the explanation I have revealed the second use I often make of the typographical resources made available to me by any moderately well-endowed word processor and an appropriately constructed printer. The italics indicate, again by convention, that the word *how* near the end of the previous paragraph is to be treated as object and not as symbol; that I am considering the word at that moment not in terms of what it means but in terms of what it is.

The word processor permits me to do so without interrupting the steady flow of my typing, once I get to know the code my word processor will recognize as an instruction to underline or italicize, as the case may be. Indeed, I have other resources as well, such as **boldface**, which for the moment I choose not to call upon, although if I were writing some other kind of text I very well might.

Similarly, with no fuss whatever I can alter margins and spacing, indent or undent (the latter a barbarous word, but it is in my word processor's vocabulary if not in mine), and in fact force my machinery to jump through as many typographical hoops as I may choose. Most of these devices contribute to lucidity. A few for the moment may not, since devices not in common use are distracting when they are first encountered.

With my customary disregard for etymology, I think of all these devices as punctuation. I shall deal with punctuation in its own terms, as well as the word processor's terms, as we proceed. It is not the most profound or interesting aspect of the written word, but it has an importance of its own, and ought not to be scorned.

It is possible to adopt the view that an excessive reliance on punctuation reveals inadequacies in the writer, who relies on such prostheses to accomplish what his own skill in writing does not stretch to managing with linguistic devices alone. I have a certain sympathy with that view, but a far greater urge for lucidity, and elegance for the sake of elegance does not attract me.

Some of this, I am sure, reflects my own personal history. My first responsible employment was in radio, where I wrote a program of which I intend to say nothing further, except that it went on the network each weekday morning and called for the services of some half dozen actors and actresses. They all showed up each morning approximately half an hour before air time for their first encounter with the script I had composed the afternoon before, and which they would perform in thirty minutes time. Half of them were quite drunk; the other half, I am proud to say, were not, but were badly hung over. Under those circumstances, I felt obliged to use every device I could imagine to assist them in reading their lines, and sprinkled punctuation amid my prose like a glutton sugaring strawberries. It helped, and I tend to overpunctuate to this day.

I practice overpunctuation, although I do not defend it. But the word processor, I believe, will in time change our perceptions of what constitutes overpunctuation. Its typographical power is enormous, and our own drive for efficiency will not let it go unused. It is impossible to say now what will be thought excessive and what reasonable, but change of some kind will surely come about.

Having delivered myself of this paean to the word processor, I feel obliged to say that I have made it all sound easier than it really is. For one thing, the business of designing word processors is in flux, like the business of designing automobiles earlier in the century. There are perhaps twenty first-rate word-processing programs offered for sale, no one of them quite like any other; it is as if every typewriter one was likely to encounter had a different arrangement of the keyboard (as to a limited extent they still do; but limited, thank heavens). Electronics matures faster than metal-bashing, fortunately, and standardization may come more rapidly.

Because word processors can accomplish so much, it is not entirely child's play to become efficient in their use, and since the computer speaks languages of its own, many of which sound ex-

actly like English but are really not, learning is a frustrating experience until that glorious day when revelation descends upon the
acolyte. During the learning period, moreover, several hours of
hard labor will inevitably be lost from time to time because the
wrong key was pressed, or the right key was not pressed, or the
local utility abruptly stopped shipping out electricity for a thou-
sandth of a second. All that will pass. All but the shortcomings of
the local utility, and even when the electricity fails only a relatively small portion of the labor will be lost.

I have written all this to relieve myself of the sense of awkward-
ness that has been passing over me each time I have referred to
the word processor in earlier pages. I shall be shameless about it
hereafter. I am only being realistic about these matters. I myself
could not conceive of continuing to write without a word processor, which on the face of it may mean no more than that I am
hopelessly eccentric or impressionable. But I know no writer—
literally none—who has encountered the word processor and not
embraced it.

I should emphasize, if I have not already done so sufficiently,
that use of the word processor imposes no fundamental change in
the act of writing. In any respect that is at all important, the writer
continues to do exactly what he has been accustomed to doing. He
is a writer still, and no machine is telling him what to write; he is
still master of his fate and captain of his soul and can sail wherever
he chooses, but now he has augmented his crew. I will enter here
only the minimum statement: He will write as well as he ever
wrote. But I believe more than that: He will write better, just as
a man driving a modern car drives better than a man in a 1908
Oldsmobile. The word processor is a marvelous machine, and no
sensible writer, if such there be, should scorn it.

Chapter Seven

Up the Ladder

Shall quips and sentences and these paper
bullets of the brain awe a man from the
career of his humor?

WILLIAM SHAKESPEARE, Much Ado About Nothing

WE MUST now abandon the security of computer languages, where everything says what it means and means what it says, and where the problem is not one of understanding but one of correspondence. We shall once more be scrambling up the ladder of complexity, hopeful if not entirely confident that lucidity is to be found somewhere up above.

In moving first from the alphabet to the word, we may be said to have moved from the artifact to the fact. The alphabet is purely an invention of man, quite arbitrary, and successful only to the extent that it serves his purposes, which it more or less does. Considered purely as a symbol, a word is likely also to be arbitrary. History may shed a certain amount of light to help explain why a Frenchman says *pain* and we say *bread,* but it does no more than cite earlier history. More fundamentally, both words exist because man has found it useful to invent a certain configuration of grain and whatnot, and requires some fashion of alluding to it when it is not in his immediate neighborhood. What that fashion may be is pretty much up to him and consequently will differ from place to place, constrained only by the fact that man is comfortable making certain noises and uncomfortable making others.

Meaning comes with the word, but the sentence is an invention that enables the speaker to compound meaning. It links words together in a manner that makes the whole a great deal more than the sum of the parts, and the increment comes out of the man-made rules of combination, just as bread itself comes out of man-made rules of combination.

The task of grappling with the universe as it manifests itself to our senses and becomes entangled with our central nervous system is encountered at the level of the sentence. To meet so immense a challenge the bare word is simply not sufficient. I have described the sentence as a device that links words together, and of course it is. But such a description applies properly to the written sentence, and the sentence lies first in the spoken language, where it is capable of linking a great deal more than words. The spoken sentence is a human construct that is not bound by the meager resources of the alphabet as the written language must be bound; it can employ all the resources of the spoken and the performed language, and most of the time it does. At the level of the sentence the task of the writer becomes formidable: he is obliged to map manner of speech and performance with nothing to rely upon but the alphabet and a variety of typographical devices.

Let us consider the simplest of assertions—I say "assertion" rather than "sentence" because I do not wish to slip into circularity or we will all become dizzy.

John gave the book to Mary.

That is, of course, a written sentence. We suspect that from the very start, because of the period.

As a written sentence, it clearly possesses what might be called a meaning, since it clearly signifies that someone named John transferred from his own possession to that of someone named Mary an object which we would all of us be likely to agree can reasonably be denominated a *book*. Indeed, it can be regarded as a standard mapping of a spoken sentence into a written sentence, and the pause that generally concludes a spoken statement is represented by the period. Nothing could be more straightforward.

Unfortunately, that written sentence provides no more than a clue, and an extremely bare clue at that, to whatever it may have been that the sentence was intended to convey. It is not too much to say that the written sentence standing there on the page, in splendid isolation, is utterly meaningless.

If we go back to the spoken sentence it is intended to map, it may have been that the speaker would have pronounced the word *John* with considerably more emphasis than the word that followed, and then paused noticeably, to emphasize the emphasis. Voice it that way, and a meaning is clear. To map that meaning and no other into the written language, some device must be found. It can be typographical:

John gave the book to Mary.

Which calls attention to the word *John* just as the emphasis did. Or:

It was John who gave the book to Mary.

Or:

John and no one but John gave the book to Mary.

If you trouble to voice either of those latter two representations, you will notice that in each instance the word *John* was firmly emphasized. The form of the sentence imposed that emphasis upon you; neither sentence would be voiced flatly without great effort. Indeed, in the second of the two the emphasis is doubled, and the sentence might be written

<u>John</u>, and no one <u>but</u> John, gave the book to Mary.

Using no more than typography, even further changes can be made in the sentence:

John gave <u>the</u> book to Mary.
John gave the <u>book</u> to Mary.
John gave the <u>book</u> to <u>Mary</u>.

Only the word *to* resists. But that may be a deficiency of my own capacity to handle unvoiced language, for I would not want to challenge Laurence Olivier's ability to ring changes by manipulating even so lowly a word as an innocuous preposition.

It would all be complex enough if it ended there, but of course it does not. If the simple sentence I have chosen to make my point should be accompanied by a smile, and certainly if it were accompanied by a leer, its significance might change beyond anything that the unexceptional words alone could possibly suggest. (In that instance, change would no doubt be created as well by the context in which the words appeared, but that much is as true of the written word as of the spoken word.) Indeed, perceivable muscular changes in any part of the body, accompanied or not by significant bodily changes, may alter the meaning of the simplest sentence; consider what goes on when a person indulges in sarcasm.

It becomes questionable whether the very phrase "spoken language" is a fair description of what is going on. Much of the burden of meaning is carried by the words, and indeed if anything complex is to be said the words are essential. But in most instances the spoken word is associated with performance even when there is no one to witness the performance: that is to say, when the speaker is in the act of talking to himself and presumably knows what he is saying even in the absence of an accompanying leer.

(The more customary reference to the performance that takes place when a conversation is carried over the telephone or its equivalent is somewhat misleading. To be sure, the listener does not see the accompanying smile or frown, but both involve specific muscular changes which in turn have their own effects upon sound production. In some sense the sound is "seen" because the smile or frown is perceived, consciously or not.)

The resources of the performed language, which include the spoken word, are truly enormous. During the missile crisis of 1962 Dean Rusk remarked, at one critical moment, "I think the other fellow just blinked." It was a metaphor, but it represented the fact that at moments a mere blink can say more than all the words at a man's command. In all likelihood, when Mr. Rusk spoke those words his colleagues heaved soundless sighs of relief, and today when Mr. Rusk recollects the event he accompanies the tale with a most informative smile.

Since the written word can neither blink, sigh, nor smile, the burden of making up for those and other deficiencies falls upon the writer, and he must be mindful of it when he writes, and even more mindful every moment when he revises; indeed, it is the principal task of revision if his first draft was preceded by any serious planning. He is not without resources.

What a speaker employs to convey information is not so much sound as change of sound. The only information directly conveyed by a steady drone is the information that someone or something is droning steadily, a fact which is not likely to command the attention for very long.

The speaker changes tempo, pitch and volume, varying all three as his message dictates. Speaking casually, he manages all this without conscious thought. But he will invoke those changes with considerable artfulness if speaking is his profession. A lecturer, a member of the reverend clergy, a politician, an actor, an anchorman—all of them are in one way or another performers by trade. (An actor is likely to be better at it than the rest, if only because an actor tends to believe what he is saying.) The changes that are rung on tempo, pitch and volume as the artful speaker proceeds are sometimes subtle changes and sometimes gross, and in either case can have a powerful effect upon meaning.

To a considerable degree, tempo, pitch and volume can all be controlled by the written word. It was by means of a careful choice of words that Browning produced the following extraordinary lines:

> Irks care the crop-full bird?
> Frets doubt the maw-crammed beast?

It must be read, aloud or silently, at the pace he intended; one might strangle reading it otherwise. It also means something, although not very much.

Similarly, vowel sounds pretty much force their natural pitch on the reader. Where long *o*'s predominate, the pitch imposed on the speaker is likely to be higher than his normal pitch and hence to draw attention—his own or that of the listener—to the words. Linguists speak of the "schwa," which is little more than a grunt separating consonants, such as the word *a* in "in a minute." When it predominates, the schwa converts unvoiced speech into unvoiced drone. It is highly soporific, if that is what the writer wants.

We have already noted the increase in volume and hence in emphasis that a writer stimulates by underlining. There are other methods that do the trick more imaginatively, such as the use of what I shall call flags: words which may have no discernible meaning themselves but warn the reader that there is significance in the offing, and to watch out for it. "Indeed" is a good example of such a word: the difference between "John is happy" and "John is indeed happy" is clear. A good writer has at hand a gaudy display of such flags, but he must call upon them sparingly, for like any stylistic device, any one of them loses all its value if it is encountered too often.

There is also cadence, which is far more important to the writer than anything I have so far discussed. But it is also more subtle, for it lies in the combination of pitch and tempo and volume, and other devices as well. I would prefer to put it off for a few moments.

In all I have been saying insidious traps lie concealed. My point has been that tempo and pitch and volume impose meaning on the reader. But it is equally true that meaning, which is what the writer is trying to convey, imposes tempo and pitch and volume. When the writer writes, he intends to manipulate tempo and pitch and volume and thereby govern the communication over which, as writer, he is bold enough to preside. He may fail to recognize that the meaning of what he wishes to communicate is instead governing him.

I am being dreadfully obscure, but fortunately I can readily illustrate my point. Norman Mailer is a practiced writer. I am among those who are not convinced that he knows <u>what</u> to write, but it is clear he knows <u>how</u> to write. His most recent novel, as of just now, contains the following sentence: "Pain is near that will be like no pain at all." As Mr. Mailer wrote that sentence, he heard it. The first three words were distinct and clear and evenly spaced in time; the next three were much diminished; the tempo slowed a bit with "like" and the last four words were upbeat again, like the first three. All very satisfying.

Except that no one reading the sentence for the first time would be likely to voice it that way. The nature of the word "that," when the word arrives, is unspecified. I must admit I am not entirely up on the jargon of the grammarian, but clearly *that* has many uses, in some of which it must be stressed while in others it is little more than a schwa. Indeed, the locution "near that," which are the words Mailer juxtaposed, is more often than not followed by such a word as "place," in which case either "that" is stressed or all three words are spoken more or less alike. Mailer clearly heard it unstressed. The resulting state of uncertainty in the reader is entirely justified, and he will be unable to voice the sentence at all, and accordingly will not understand the sentence for some considerable length of time. That is not lucidity. When he comes to understand it, by the way, he will be unable to recreate his uncertainty, since once meaning and the words themselves have been wedded it is most difficult to put them asunder, just as an optical puzzle of the sort found in psychology texts vanishes forever once the puzzle is resolved.

(Writer at work: The final sentence in the paragraph above, when I first wrote it, began "When he does understand it . . ." As I <u>wrote</u> it I <u>heard</u> it, and it was crystal clear. When I came to reread it, I suspected at once that the word "does" was floating; I heard it stressed, but there was nothing to indicate that stress to the reader. No problem. It was as easy to correct as it was to write it incorrectly in the first place.)

The obligation all this imposes on the writer is as wearing as anything he confronts. No matter how thoroughly he understands his sentence, he must never abandon an awareness that he may himself be deceived by what he hears in his head as he writes and even by what he hears in his head when he reads what he writes. Without conscious effort he will never suspect that another reader may impose on his words a quite different sound, and thereby draw from his words a quite different meaning or, perhaps more frequently, be forced to struggle to elicit any relevant meaning at all.

I can put it off no longer, and must now speak of cadence. A sentence as a whole—any sentence—can be regarded as a flow of sound which begins with something of a pause and ends with something of a pause. It is not quite that, of course, but near enough for never mind. The pattern of that flow of sound I call the cadence of the sentence, the consequence of tempo and pitch and volume. Cadence should in principle be graceful and easy; the sentence should sing. But it is not quite as simple at that, for what we are driving for is the communication of meaning, and in those instances where the meaning itself is graceless, so should be the cadence. The quotation above from Browning is an example. Not the best of all examples, for it calls a good deal too much attention to itself and one hears the creak of the machinery. It is a caricature of good expository writing and not a fair picture, but since Browning had not set out to compose expository writing he may be forgiven.

I confess that I am at a loss to say much more about cadence. I am not sure how it is created, or how it is lost. I am not even sure how it can be recognized when it is encountered. But there is no doubt at all in my mind that some writers are easier to read than others, even though they may use less familiar words and more intricate constructions, and that a good part of that achievement lies in the cadence of their prose. Not all, I hasten to add. But enough to make a real difference. I can recognize, too, the writer with a tin ear, although when I try to justify that impression to others I tend to sputter. Still, it is ease and grace we are talking about, and as far as I know there is no one who has ever said clearly exactly what it is that constitutes ease and grace.

Cadence also implies variety. The ear wearies of a tune endlessly repeated, however attractive the tune may be. There comes a time when we wish to hear no more of the César Franck symphony, much though it charmed us at the outset. But this carries us outside the bounds of the sentence, into the high grass of the paragraph and beyond, and we must be orderly about all this.

We have been flying fairly high, and we must return to terra firma, where we can look at the written sentence somewhat more formally, and search out its more mundane resources.

If a definition was required of me—and I must say that up to now no one has ever asked me—I would say that a written sentence is an assemblage of words that either asserts a complete proposition of some kind or another, or warns that such a proposition is in the making and will shortly be along. I should add that in this context an assemblage of one is quite legitimate: "Stop!" is a sentence. What a spoken sentence may be I cannot say and I am not prepared to try.

That is not what we were taught in grade school. It would be difficult for any of us to recall exactly <u>what</u> we were taught, but there was gabble about subjects and objects and predicates; nominatives and accusatives; compound and complex; and much more of the same. It was all designed to enable the teacher to scrawl in red pencil, somewhere in the margin of our submission, "Not a sentence!" which now that I come to think of it was itself not a sentence, according to her own criteria. Strange: it never occurred to me at the time.

In any case, the only criterion for a sentence is that it complete a thought of some kind. It may be an isolated thought, but it is equally likely to be a completed thought only in the context of neighboring sentences, which means that while it is possible to examine an assemblage of words in isolation and say decisively that it constitutes a sentence, it is frequently impossible to examine such an assemblage and say with confidence that it does not.

For an extreme instance, examine if you will five consecutive lines of dialogue from Shakespeare's <u>King John</u>. They read, in their entirety, as follows:

> K. JOHN. Death.
> HUBERT.   My Lord?
> K. JOHN.   The grave.
> HUBERT.   He shall not live.
> K. JOHN.   Enough.

To be sure, those lines were written to be spoken aloud, and they represent as closely as the written word can do so the spoken word. But as a matter of fact, <u>King John</u> has never been a smash hit on stage and the words are far more often read than heard. And as written language, even in isolation from the context of the play, they have impact. Among the five lines, they can boast only one verb, and not much of anything else; it is difficult to locate any one of them, except the fourth, within a traditional definition of *sentence*. They can be smuggled in, one way or another: called "sentence fragments"; or elliptical, after which the missing words are provided and King John is now credited with having said: "[I want him put to] death." But to do so is to play ducks and drakes with common sense: they are sentences, or the very word *sentence* has lost all useful meaning.

They come in all shapes and forms. There are short sentences; not as short as those just quoted but short enough to be distinguishably so. There are sentences that only sound short. I quote from Voltaire's Candide, written in French, to be sure, but a book that translates well:

> The next day after dinner, upon leaving the table, Cunegonde and Candide found themselves behind a screen; Cunegonde dropped her handkerchief, Candide picked it up, she innocently took his hand, the young man innocently kissed the hand of the young girl with spirit, sensibility, a very special grace; their mouths met, their eyes flamed, their knees trembled, their hands wandered.

It is wonderfully effective writing, in which the series of short spurts of language catapults the reader along exactly as Candide and Cunegonde were hurtling along to exactly where they both wanted to go. How such a sentence would be classified I simply do not know. Or care.

And then there are long sentences, of which, as I recall it, perhaps the longest is to be found in one of John Donne's Sermons, where it must have begun at about eleven o'clock of a fine Sunday morning and gone on until very near noon. I recall reading it when I was very young and given to such fripperies, but I do not now have that sentence at hand, and I blanch at the prospect of reading Donne's religious writings in their entirety in order to find it again. The principle is clear enough: a simple grammatical structure is iterated and reiterated, and finally broken. As for example:

> If you eat nourishing food from earliest youth, if you devote all your waking hours to leaping up and down, if you learn to run repeatedly thirty yards or so back and forth without losing speed on the turns, if you can win admission to a state university or Notre Dame, then and only then you too can become a professional basketball player.

I am being frivolous. But sentences of that sort, thoughtfully drafted and in their proper place, can constitute wonderfully effective writing. Such a sentence—a periodic sentence, it is called in the textbooks—accumulates power as it goes; it hammers at the reader; at the same time it lays down a trail of clues, and there is never much doubt where it is going.

We can honor as well the artful sentence. A very famous sample, from Thomas B. Macaulay's History of England:

> The Puritans objected to bear baiting, not because it gave pain to the bears but because it gave pleasure to the spectators.

A balanced sentence, technically, for obvious reasons, not that it matters. Macaulay used them constantly, and thereby achieved a general sense of stateliness at the price of some ennui, which accompanies stateliness wherever it occurs.

Still another kind of sentence is worth considering. It might be called an echoic sentence (or an echoic style) and achieves its effect by imposing upon the reader a recollection of other sentences with which he can be relied upon to be familiar, whether consciously or not. John Livingston Lowes's The Road to Xanadu is an unbroken stream of sentences reminiscent of Coleridge, and since the book itself deals with Coleridge, produces a feeling of authenticity. I myself overemploy phrases from Shakespeare, or close to phrases from Shakespeare, for reasons I do not entirely understand. Envy, probably.

My favorite example, however, goes back a long way, when a writer named Kahlil Gibran unaccountably flourished and was even revered by adolescent girls. (I am not sure he was really named Kahlil Gibran, but his books were so signed.) Gibran, or whoever, had mastered the art of writing very much like the translators of the King James Bible, and the language of that Bible is deeply embedded in every one of us who speaks English, not excepting heathens, with all the overtones one might expect. It was impossible to discern any interesting meaning in anything Gibran wrote, but the borrowed tone made it all sound holy, if nothing else, and he had at least one runaway best-seller.

Oratory, by the way, and particularly black oratory, employs the very same device. It was enormously effective for Martin Luther

King, Jr., for it was a language that transcended the enormous differences and disputes that divided the races, and with that language he reached blacks and whites alike.

That brief digression leads somehow to a consideration of one form of pathological sentence, in which a series of more or less independent statements is strung together with *and*s to make a long, wearisome sentence of its own. The practice is not very serious in the spoken language, where "and" serves much the purpose of the period in the written word. In such instances, "and" is never really spoken, but is more nearly a small noise made by the speaker as he pauses and prepares for the sentence to come. In the written word, however, *and* has a meaning of its own, just as it has in the spoken word when it is enunciated: it is used to couple, and if coupling of some sort is not to be conveyed, the word should not be used.

A pathology less readily detected, and more widely disseminated, is flabby sentence structure, characterized above all by words that do not pull their weight. Worst of all, the more practiced the writer, the more flab prone he is likely to be; the words simply flow, whether they mean anything or not.

Conventional wisdom has it that sentences cast in the passive mode are ipso facto flabby, and the conventional wisdom is pretty much right. The preceding sentence originally began "It is the conventional wisdom that . . ." No more need be said. Yet even here, judgment must be exercised. There are times when the passive mode is required if meaning is to be clearly communicated, and to shun it under those circumstances is as much a fault as its needless employment.

Leaving aside the pathologies, any form of sentence is quite as respectable as any other, whether it is long or short, simple or complex. There exists a basic sentence form, which consists of a noun, a verb, and an adjective or another noun, and a fine form it is. But the basic sentence form is like a woman's basic black costume, to be worn when she isn't doing anything in particular but would like to be properly dressed.

In short, there are many kinds of sentence, among them kinds that are radically different. In certain situations, such as the preparation of a scholarly report or a legal document, a distinct and unalterable form is imposed upon the writer, and he is expected to abide by it. To the extent that he has choice, however, he should be prepared to exercise it, and exercise it widely. That kind of choice is at the heart of his craft. The professional pitcher is most effective if he has at his command a fast ball, a curve, a slider, a few off-speed pitches, and even something not entirely classifiable and all his own. He is most effective above all if he mixes them up, so that each separate pitch is in some degree unexpected. Something very much like that constitutes the craft of the writer, except that while it is unwise to smear grease on his manuscript before he delivers it, there is no hard-and-fast rule against it.

I have now come very near the end of a long disquisition on the sentence without so much as a mention of syntax, even though it is syntax that makes most sentences anything more than random collections of letters and words. All in good time.

The sentence, after all, is part of the paragraph; the paragraph may be part of a chapter, the chapter part of a section, the section part of a book or a report, and on and on until we come to some collective noun that represents part of the Library of Congress. There is far more to be said about the sentence than is to be found in this chapter, but it goes somewhat beyond the sentence itself into the higher domains, which we have yet to penetrate.

Chapter Eight

Points at Issue

I just love dropping in them commas.

HOMER BIGART (in late evening conversation)

AFTER having dealt with such elegant matters as tempo and cadence, we can scarcely escape some sort of descent to the humdrum. Inescapable: there are nuts and bolts to be tended. It seems a pity. There is a good deal of satisfaction to be had from placing what appears to be exactly the right word exactly where it manifestly belongs. More than satisfaction; positively elation. Making a decisive choice between semicolons and commas does not lift the spirits in quite the same degree, particularly when the task is performed in the full knowledge that most of them will have to be extracted later.

Punctuation, like the alphabet, is to be found in written language alone, and might very well be looked upon as an extension of the alphabet. No illumination is provided by examining the uses of punctuation in the computer, where it is a quite different matter and to some extent has gone its own way. Indeed, one of the best-known higher-level computer languages uses a semicolon to signify the end of a sentence, although why it has chosen to do so I do not know. More generally, the novice in almost any higher-level computer language is likely to have more trouble with punctuation than with the language itself, since it is not punctuation at all as he understands it, but a somewhat elaborate code in its own right. The programmer has taken advantage of the presence of certain keys on the standard typewriter keyboard, and that is all. I speak now of computer languages in general; word processing is another matter, where the comma means what the good Lord meant it to mean, at least most of the time.

As indicated above, I have taken some liberties with the word *punctuation.* What it has come to mean to me includes not only the well-recognized dots and squiggles to which we are introduced at the earliest possible age but also the full typographical resources of the word-processing machinery and the printing mechanism that goes with it. Those resources vary from word processor to word processor, and some of them boggle the mind. After writing a paragraph, for example, with a few strokes of the keys I can convert it thus:

1. this, and go on doing it until I tell the processor
2. to stop, although it is not often that I have
3. the slightest desire to do this. Still, I suppose it
4. is comforting to know I could if I wanted to, and
5. I am sure someday I will want to.

The purpose of all this, of course, is to provide the writer with greater and more powerful weapons with which to battle opacity. Punctuation, in general, is employed to guide the reader as he voices the words he is reading. It is almost always needed in the written word, and sometimes badly needed. It is almost always used, and sometimes badly used.

For the most part, the counterpart to any given sample of punctuation is what would be a change of tempo or pitch or volume in the spoken language. The period, for example, invariably signals a distinct pause, not very much extended. In addition, the voice level generally falls somewhat, although professional speakers usually train themselves not to let that happen for fear that some priceless portion of the utterance be lost on the hearer.

By convention, the period concludes a sentence. A sentence, whether one word or two pages long, carries a sense of completion, and it is helpful if that completion is made known to the listener. A pause seems a quite natural way to do so, and there is little more that can be said about it. The period, however, is a good deal more arbitrary than the simple pause. Voicing the written language, you will find that the pause represented by the period is not significantly different from the pause represented by the comma. The rule is that a period is used to conclude a sentence, a comma used within a sentence. That is a special device available to the writer but not to the speaker, who must handle problems of the sort by the manner in which he governs volume. Punctuation provides several instances of that sort, which is splendid, for we writers need all the edge we can get.

The comma is every bit as simple as the period, but the pedagogues have made it into a mystification. Again, it is the written equivalent of a distinct pause generally accompanied by a fall in volume and pitch. That is all it is.

Observe the following two sentences, properly garnished with commas, or without them.

The boy who is tall walks down the street.
The boy, who is tall, walks down the street.

Guided by the commas in voicing those sentences, one is immediately aware of the difference in meaning. I will not state the difference; to do so is entirely superfluous. We all learned it when we learned to speak.

To deal with this the grammarians have invented such concepts as the dependent clause and the independent clause and relative pronouns and no doubt distinctions even further refined. Those concepts, and others like them, are useful to the scholar; they make possible an orderly study of language. They do not help at all while one writes. They are pedagogically insane. A child, or for all that an adult, is asked first to ferret out the clause (whatever that may be), then to determine whether it seems to be dependent or independent, and finally, if he can keep in his mind which is which, to insert commas or not, as the case may be. All he needs to know is that whenever he would pause slightly in speaking a sentence he had better stick in a comma when he writes it. Learning, he will make mistakes, but at least they will be clear-cut, comprehensible mistakes.

Sooner or later pedagogy creates rules which do violence to language itself, or obfuscate it. Thus, the sentence

Any boy who likes rock music should get himself a stereo.

clearly needs no comma, while

Any boy who likes rock music when it is played by someone who understands rock music, should get himself a stereo.

needs one badly. The first is necessarily voiced without pause, the second has a pause where I have inserted the comma. Since the two sentences have the same general structure, the pedagogues are obliged to teach that they must be punctuated in the same fashion, or that the one which is obscure when punctuated "properly" should be rewritten.

I must be fair to the pedagogues; they are not utterly wrong. Sentences frequently require an abundance of commas simply because they are badly written. A little craftsmanship would get rid of both commas and obscurity. But if there must be rules they should be about that, and not about commas. Indeed, I shall make such a rule on the spot. It will be Rule No. 6.

6. At each revision of whatever a writer may be writing, he should be on guard against commas. A profusion of commas frequently signifies sentences and paragraphs that could do with further sharpening.

(It turned out to be Rule No. 6 because I am showing off my word processor, which keeps track of how much numbering has been going on. Since I have used lines numbered 1 to 5 earlier, when I ask for another line to be numbered, my computer, which has sneakily kept track, gives me number 6. If you are wondering, I can assure you that there are no Rules No. 1 to 5, and there will be no Rule No. 7 or above.)

I myself overpunctuate wildly, probably for the reason I pointed out earlier, although it may only be that my genes are badly tangled or something of that general sort. Much of it goes away when I revise, and a good deal more when I am edited. As a practical matter, I think it wise to overpunctuate, so long as Rule No. 6 is scrupulously heeded, for it leads to careful examination of a good many sentences, some of which can be improved even if the punctuation passes muster.

The semicolon indicates a pause somewhat longer than that of the period or comma. In the spoken language, a distinct change in the direction that a discourse has been taking requires a fairly substantial pause. What that unmistakable pause says to the listener is something like the following: "Pay attention, now. What I shall say next is not completely a pursuit of what I have just finished saying."

The semicolon's use in the written word, aside from a technical use in listings, is more easily illustrated than described, and for the illustration I go back to Joseph Hobbs, who taught me English at high school and who had managed to compress all useful information about the semicolon into one brief autobiographical sentence: "I used to live in Allston; now I live in Belmont." As Mr. Hobbs pointed out, the first half of that sentence carries the implication that the speaker is about to consider some aspect or another of life in Allston, which is simply not the case. On the other hand, there is a close enough connection between the two halves to make it reasonable to present them, within the written word, as one, since the sentence as a whole indicates that Mr. Hobbs had moved up in the world, and none of that meaning is to be found in either half alone. Hence the semicolon.

It is as much convention as punctuation. The necessary pause could be provided in other ways:

I used to live in Allston. Now I live in Belmont.

would do. The semicolon says a bit more.

The colon has in effect ceased to be a punctuation mark at all and become a symbol in its own right. It was not always so. As an admirer of Charles Dickens in good standing, I own a facsimile of his handwritten A Christmas Carol, which begins:

Marley was dead: to begin with.

Clearly, to Dickens the colon indicated a quite substantial pause, introduced into the spoken language for effect and (in the form of the colon) into the written language for the same purpose. Either that, or it was a slip of the pen, which hardly seems conceivable.

These days it is simply shorthand for *to wit* (and I must remember someday to look up *to wit*). It is used to preface an explicit series of items, which are then separated conventionally by semicolons, or a less explicit series of parallel statements of one kind or another, which are also separated by semicolons, or as in:

He is foolish: he uses colons.

I tend to scatter them freely when I write, and take them all out when I revise. I find it excellent exercise. Once in a while, I permit one to survive and the editor takes it out.

The question mark and exclamation point are generally included in any respectable list of punctuation marks, which is quite reasonable. There is nothing very much to be said about them, except that they give pitch and volume instructions to the reader, which are quite explicit where the question mark is concerned and less so for the exclamation point. Spanish-speaking folks print them upside down at the beginning of a sentence as well as right side up at the end, which seems to me to be quite intelligent, since for the exclamation point in particular it is good to be able to anticipate it. Neither necessarily indicates the end of a sentence, and

Are you amused? you really shouldn't be.

is quite effective. The question mark gives pitch, and it makes sense to insert it where the instruction takes effect. But the assemblage of words as a whole is clearly a single sentence, for it is voiced pretty much without pause.

The voicing produced by the question mark is irreplaceable in the written word. I quoted earlier from <u>King John</u>:

K. JOHN. Death.
HUBERT.   My Lord?
K. JOHN.   The grave.
HUBERT.   He shall not live.
K. JOHN.   Enough.

Oddly enough, in the First Folio Hubert's first response is written

My Lord.

and was changed by later editors. Writing it so relieves the actor of the obligation imposed on him by the question mark. He might well choose instead to read the line

My Lord!

which is quite a different matter. I have no idea what Shakespeare intended.

As I have been going about my business, my sense of the absurd has been whispering to me and I think it is time I gave it heed. I have been insistent about the coupling between the written word and the rhythms of speech, and it is all somewhat reminiscent of that fine musical comedy <u>The Music Man</u>, where the hero created a virtuoso boys' band by urging the boys, none of whom had theretofore so much as touched a musical instrument, to "think the Minuet in G." The similarity amuses me but does not concern me, since thinking about the sousaphone and actually playing one are distinctly different activities, and it is not very useful to think much about the sousaphone until after you have learned to play it, at which point thinking about the Minuet in G might be extremely productive.

I do not intend to pursue conventional punctuation much farther. I have omitted any mention of dashes and parentheses and quotation marks and I suspect much else. Handbooks will tell you how, in general, they are used, and your own unvoiced speech will tell you why. The latter is a better guide than the former. I am always somewhat annoyed when a speaker says "quote" or "quote, unquote": the sound of his voice will always do that job for him.

Taking the liberties I advertised, I consider spaces to be punctuation marks, excepting the spaces that surround individual words. Typists and some word processors insert double spaces after sentences, to hint at a pause somewhat longer than the pause indicated by a comma. A paragraph is surrounded by considerable space. When a document is broken into sections, with a consequent profligate use of space, it suggests that the reader is permitted to go out for coffee; when it is broken into chapters he can put it aside overnight; when it is broken into volumes he may not be troubled with the next volume for a year or two, thus adding temporal to physical space. I shall say more about this, less flippantly, when we begin to think about the written word in broader terms. Meanwhile I shall insert a somewhat larger space than usual between the end of this paragraph and the next, for good reason.

The ease with which the word processor, coupled with a moderately sophisticated printer, manipulates typography makes it likely that there will be further codification. Writing all this, for example, I have carefully observed distinctions in the use I make of quotation marks, the underline, and italics. Quotation marks have been used to signify what someone actually said or wrote.

They are commonly used, from time to time, to signify that a word or phrase is to be taken in a somewhat unusual sense, but that usage is so shamelessly abused that any prudent writer will pass it through the sieve at least three times before he dares. Underlines, when they are not being used for emphasis, usually indicate the name of something but not someone, for in the latter case they are not necessary. Italics indicate that a word is being considered as an object and not in terms of its meaning, so that I may write "I use *never* to mean occasionally."

There are still other resources, although as I proceed I fear it becomes less and less reasonable to call them forms of punctuation, even though they contribute as punctuation contributes. Even more than any of those I have so far considered, they are the resources of the word processor.

I am able, for example, to summarize my views on the use of punctuation in the following form:

- No writer may employ elaborate punctuation unless he is twelve years old or older.
- Punctuation that begins on one page and continues into a second should be considered excessive.
- If semicolons are called for, both the top and bottom halves should be written.
- The fact that a question mark is a most attractive symbol does not justify its use in declarative sentences.

Nonsense or not, set down in that fashion or something like it, those remarks are easy to read and give the momentary impression of orderly thought, which would be likely to endure if they meant anything at all. The word processor made that typographical arrangement painless, and it is worth mentioning that it was managed by a word-processing program that is not at all elaborate. I have another at my command that is capable of gymnastics beyond belief. It almost wearies me to think of it.

If it all seems more a display of electronic virtuosity than an aspect of the writing craft, I can only point out that in every instance the purpose has been to enhance lucidity. Each one of the devices I have lumped together—even the last of them—either assists the reader in approximating the voice that underlies the written word, or eases the labors of the eye as it governs the decoding process. That last sentence includes dashes, which are not in the catalogue of punctuation so far considered, nor are parentheses, but there is surely no need to labor the central point: all of what I am calling punctuation, even the use of numbered lines far back in these pages, can be "heard" if the sentences are voiced. At times the change in the sound of the spoken sentence is subtle, but it is always there.

There are certainly those who consider a reliance upon punctuation to be the mark of a lazy writer, and there is a great deal to be said for that view. Punctuation certainly can be abused as well as misused. But some punctuation is indispensable, as even the purists will agree, and it seems sensible to give consideration to where the line should be drawn rather than issue outright condemnations of anything but the most basic punctuation marks and their most pedestrian uses.

In this instance as in so many others, an awareness of writing as process comes into play. First drafts are best written headlong, in order to get the material in a form which permits easy handling. A certain kind of sculptor, possessed of a huge block of Carrara marble and some image of what he would like to make of it, begins with a process of banging away before he gets down to the fine strokes. The writer is even better positioned; at least he can comfort himself with the realization that his early errors can be rectified.

Written headlong, excessive punctuation has great virtues. It is by no means unusual to be confronted with a sentence or even a paragraph that even its author no longer understands. Punctuation, blunt weapon though it may be, brings back the sound that underlay the written word, and makes it possible to recover the significance of the maimed words and phrases.

In that sense, much of it is scaffolding which should be torn down as the work proceeds. Where words and their arrangement can do the work, they should be permitted to do so; if a sentence is abundantly clear without anything more than conventional punctuation—the period at the end of the sentence—it should be written that way. But even in the finished product there is no need to choose between excess and abnegation, any more than a man must choose between well water and Muscatel drunk out of a brown bag. Of the two I much prefer well water, but I do not scorn fine wine with dinner or even a martini or two when the occasion calls for it.

Driven by technology, the written word may well evolve in the direction of typographical variety. It will be the ease that will do it. Everything done here with the word processor can be done without it. But it is most difficult to achieve on the old-fashioned typewriter, and requires an intensity of attention that must be stolen from attention required simply to get things down on paper. It was actually easier to be extravagant typographically with pen or pencil or quill, and there was more of that sort of thing in those days. But it begins to seem that what technology hath given away technology hath been good enough to hand back.

If that is so, it is futile to whine about it. In any case, I have no disposition to do so, for on balance I believe that the judicious use of the resources of technology, here as elsewhere, is the way to go. I raise at least two cheers for IBM.

Chapter Nine

Interlude

This is a gift I have, simple, simple; a foolish
extravagant spirit, full of forms, figures,
shapes, objects, ideas, apprehensions,
motions, revolutions. . . . But the gift is good
in those in whom it is acute, and I am
thankful for it.

WILLIAM SHAKESPEARE, <u>Love's Labour's Lost</u>

WE ARE a long way along, in bulk at least, and still have not really begun to get to the heart of the matter. In a strict sense we have not yet been dealing at all with the written word itself, but rather with the tools that we have at our command when any of us sit at the word processor or the typewriter or the lined yellow pad, which is not the same thing at all. To revert once more to the metaphor I find most handy, we have laid out the chisels and the planes and the saws, but we have yet not begun to build anything. It might be useful at this point to review just what those tools appear to be.

The first of them, and the most important of them all, is the spoken language. It underlies anything we may choose to write, and echoes in anything we may have written. It must be, at every stage of our endeavor, mentor and guide. As a general rule, if what we have written cannot be spoken, there is almost surely something wrong with it. A general rule and nothing more, and like all general rules it admits of exceptions. But it is where we must always begin.

This is not at all to say that the spoken and the written languages are identical. I would not speak exactly as I am writing here, and the complexity of the mapping process makes it impossible for me to write exactly as I speak. But the process of conversion I undertake when I write is a process that runs from the spoken to the written, and presupposes the spoken. I am not familiar with the problems of those who are deaf and mute from birth, nor of those few who think almost entirely in modes other than those that language provides. There may very well be constructs other than the spoken language that lead in their own way to the written language. But they do not enter into the lives of most of us: they are special problems with special solutions.

The miracle is that our primary tool, the spoken language, in all its complexity and with all its abundance, is not something we strive and struggle to master, step by step, but rather is somehow bestowed upon us, for all the world like a gift from the gods. I overstate, of course. There is a certain amount of struggling and striving, but it comes after we become consciously aware of the full complexity of the spoken language and its extraordinary scope. Long before complexity dawns upon us we are already astonishingly efficient speakers, although not necessarily very elegant speakers. When I call that a miracle, I do not overstate at all.

To a thoughtful person the very notion of the miraculous is somewhat offensive, which explains some of the agony of the professional linguist. A child of eighteen months or so is already able to communicate by means of language, and a few months later is beginning to piece together sentences which represent with considerable fidelity the extraordinarily complex syntactical practices of whatever his native language may happen to be. Looking at the matter as dispassionately as we can, we find no acts the child will perform in all his life as complex as the act of converting the present state of his neurons and synapses into coherent communication, and only *Homo sapiens* of all the innumerable species is capable of achieving it. The infant manages it with remarkable efficiency, and does so long before he has comparable command of his bowels and bladder—achievements which appear also to be pretty much unique to *Homo sapiens,* come to think of it.

Do not mistake me. Society imposes standards upon the spoken language, and I am suggesting neither that there are standards upon which there is uniform agreement within any society, nor that those standards are automatically or effortlessly met by the child, or by the adult. It is sensible to distinguish between "speaking" and "speaking well" or "speaking correctly," the last of which is a devilishly complex notion. The infant achieves neither of the last two, however they may be defined, nor do many adults. But every human who is not pathologically deficient possesses a language in which he can communicate efficiently over most of the range in which he wishes to communicate or needs to communicate, and can do so with a degree of subtlety which would be positively astounding if it were not so universal. And that very universality makes it almost impossible to appreciate the immensity of the accomplishment.

The exact manner in which the individual develops his private command of the social utility we call his native language is a matter of environment in the broadest sense of the word. (As we are all aware when we come to think of it, we all speak several varieties of our native language, as circumstances appear to dictate, but for the moment I will consider them all as an aggregate which can appropriately enough be called "the" native language.) Not to be too finicky about the matter, or to be too attentive to the exceptional cases, the child is likely to begin by speaking as his parents speak; he will be much affected after a bit by the manner of speech of those within the broadening circle of his associates, including his teachers; at a later age he may very well make conscious efforts to "improve" his spoken language. For some, although not many, there will be at some stage an interaction with the written language which may bring about distinct changes in the spoken language.

Out of all this idiosyncratic agglomeration comes the subset, or the subsets, of the spoken native language which the writer seeks to map into the written language. That spoken native language will be his principal tool. If he has a tin ear for his own language, what he writes will also be tin. Whatever the formal knowledge he may accumulate of grammar and syntax and vocabulary, or of metonymy or synecdoche or aposiopesis, or of ablative absolutes or subjunctives or transitive verbs, and however doggedly he may go about the task of accumulating even more formal knowledge, he will still write tin.

I was careful above to specify "the spoken native language which the writer seeks to map into the written language." That need not be the spoken native language that the writer ordinarily speaks, but rather one of the many subsets to which I have referred. It is my own suspicion that a professional expository writer is likely to be at his best when his written language is closest to his natural spoken language, but with so many people looking over his shoulder, that will be a luxury he will not always be able to afford, until the day comes (if it comes at all) when he no longer gives a damn.

We have considered in earlier pages the alphabet, the word, the sentence and punctuation. These, too, are tools of the written word and not its substance. This may appear to be a rather odd point of view, since among other things it places me in the position of asserting that a written word is not the written word.

The significant aspect of all those aspects of the written language is that to a large extent they can be considered in their own terms. The letter *a* can be discussed as just that and nothing more. It is no matter whether it appears in a lease or in a sentence out of Hamlet; what it is remains in every instance the letter *a* and nothing either more or less. What can be sensibly said about the letter *a* at any time can be said about any other occurrence of the letter *a* so long as it is being used as a letter. (The qualification covers those instances such as "f=ma," where *f* is not used as a letter at all but as an abbreviation physicists use to denote the concept of "force.")

Matters become slightly more complicated as we move up the scale, but still there is a great deal that can be said about a word, a sentence, or punctuation, much as we speak of letters of the alphabet. Each can be analyzed in one fashion or another entirely in its own right, although such analysis may be only partial. To a large extent, it is possible to say whether a sentence is well formed and lucid without being very much concerned with anything beyond that sentence itself; the existence of dictionaries is evidence enough of the fact that words possess a kind of independent existence of their own. Punctuation, finally, is for the most part little more than a very special kind of letter.

But consider for a moment the paragraph. Very little can be said about it except in terms of the document of which it is a part, except perhaps in the limiting case in which the paragraph is the document. Very little is not quite the same as nothing at all, and in fact whole books have been written about "The Paragraph," but what they contain is largely an alternation between triviality and tautology, none of it either interesting or useful so far as the practicing writer is concerned.

For better or for worse, I am asserting a discontinuity. The close analysis of the written word can go only so far in detail; very quickly it becomes the analysis of the document as a whole. At the moment of that discontinuity, the notion of the craftsman's tools becomes subordinate to the notion of the relationship between the tools at hand and the craftsman's larger purposes. It will be necessary, in the end, to say a great deal about the paragraph, but when I set out to do so I shall not be writing nearly so much about the paragraph itself as about its role in the larger structure.

I do not want to make too much of this right now, for I will be making a good deal of it later. But I can afford to pause and epitomize the sort of thing I have in mind. Except in the classroom, no one engaged in serious writing sets out to write either a sentence or a paragraph. What he plans to write I call, for want of a better name, a *document,* which is a neutral kind of word for any written material that has a beginning, a middle and an end, as well as some nontrivial purpose. In the course of writing a document, the author will write sentences and paragraphs, both of which are well-defined entities. But when he writes a sentence, his principal concern will be with problems of "how." When he writes a paragraph, his principal concern will be with problems of "why." In the first instance, he will be manipulating his tools; in the second, his mind. I am not aggrandizing the one and deprecating the other; he had better be able to do both.

The distinction is important. I note it here because most of what remains will be concerned with the document, and not with the details of the document.

But back to the tools we have available as we continue our search for lucidity. You have no doubt noticed that I have so far had very little to say about grammar or what is more broadly denominated syntax. I cannot imagine anyone who has not endured at the very least a dozen years of formal exposure to grammar, as well as several years in which what are known as rules of grammar were expounded at his parents' knees, since it is well known that every adult American is an ever-flowing fount of grammatical information, all of it as unarguable as the laws of the Medes and the Persians. That remarkable wealth, presumably, is the capital investment that goes into the making of a writer. It is my duty, accordingly, to deal with the matter, and I shall do so at once.

As an honest man, I shall begin by making my own views clear, if they are not clear already. Virtually all that is hammered into the student until his college years at least, and much thereafter, is presented nonsensically. That is not as lamentable as it might be, since what is being presented is itself largely nonsense, and the harmony that thus exists between content and style has a certain charm of its own. Since people by and large seem impelled to act sensibly most of the time, relatively little damage is in fact done by all this, except as it turns some small proportion of the citizenry into pedants who vigorously move about unsplitting infinitives and inserting the word *whom* where it does not belong.

Syntax in general is the set of practices which a society has adopted as part of the process of assembling words into sentences from which a meaning can be extracted. Examined closely, syntactical practices in English command, if we are to conform with the practices of our fellows, that if we wish to convey information concerning the color of a house without befuddling the person to whom we are talking or writing, we will generally be well advised to place the word denoting the color temporally or physically before the word denoting the house. We are permitted to say "the green mansion" but not "the mansion green" unless we are presuming to write poetry, in which case we may say pretty much what we please. If, however, we happen to be born in Paris, France, instead of Paris, Kentucky, we must do exactly the opposite.

As a practical matter, we learn most of this exactly as we learn the meaning of the words *green* and *mansion* themselves: by exposure. Once again, the child has learned a miraculous amount of syntax at the age of three or four, and continues to learn it for the ensuing dozen or so years whether he pays attention at school or not. And once again, the syntax he learns is a consequence of the environment or environments into which fate and chance hurl him. If he chances to be reared in what I shall call, without further discussion, a cultivated environment he will say "he doesn't." He will otherwise say "he don't," no matter what his teacher tells him, because that is what all the people he knows, with the single exception of the teacher, say. If he and the teacher both happened to have been born into cultivated circles in 1825 or thereabouts, it is likely that both of them would have customarily said "he don't," not to mention "he ain't."

I speak now of the spoken language. Many years ago Ring Lardner expressed a certain contempt for a journalistic colleague who was ghost-writing a sports column in the name of a distinguished baseball player known to be somewhat uncultivated. Under that player's signature he had written "I ain't got no objection" or something of the sort. Lardner was savage about it. It was quite true, he pointed out, that the player in question would have <u>said</u> "I ain't got no objection." But he would have <u>written</u> "I *haven't* got no objection." In that oblique fashion I make the point, to which I shall return, that the syntaxes of the spoken and the written language are two quite different syntaxes, as even a baseball player would know.

However . . .

Enter the pedagogue. Over most of history, there were no professional pedagogues, or so few as to make no great difference, although in the more general sense of the word we may be sure there were always pedagogues. So far as society in general was concerned, there were very few who were literate or likely to be, and all of them managed quite comfortably to speak a native language, syntax and all. Time passed, and movable type was invented, and the written language suddenly took on a new importance and a new dignity. A whole new market emerged, in which a living might be made by teaching people to read and write.

Restricting ourselves to the English language (although English was by no means a special case), to the pedagogues the language was an unholy mess. Whatever its roots may have been, it had been changed decade by decade for centuries, and what is more, changed in a fashion that appeared to be almost haphazard. Much of the change stemmed from one of mankind's greatest assets: man's fundamental laziness. For what reason I do not know, it appears that in the languages from which modern Western European languages arose, meaning was imposed upon a collection of words by slight changes in the words themselves. As time passed, it must have been easier to hold the words more or less constant and impose meaning primarily by the order in which they were spoken. Thus, the distinct Latin words *Amo, amas, amat, amamus, amatis, amant* have for the most part been supplanted in English (and most other languages) by a whole family of words meaning

"I" and "you" and "he" and "she" and the like which do duty
before all verbs, including the verb *love*. Much simpler.

Unfortunately, not as simple as all that. People are not only lazy;
they are also untidy. For no reason at all, we may say "I love" and
"you love" and "we" or "they" love, but we must say "he" or "she"
or even "it" *loves*. Irrational! unconscionable! sheer idiocy! No
pedagogue would willingly put up with anything of that sort.

The recourse that came first to mind was simply to derogate the
English language and make no attempt to teach it at all. Greek and
Latin grammar were taught for centuries to those who had any
formal education at all; English and French and German were
considered to be no more than debased forms of Latin, and among
the truly cultured even Latin was sometimes suspected of being
no more than a debased form of Greek.

For a short while it made a certain amount of sense. Whatever
the revisionists may pretend, Western Europe was emerging from
the Dark Ages, and what recorded knowledge there was had been
recorded or rerecorded in Latin. It was not until the sixteenth
century that a scholar dared write a learned book in, as it happened, Italian. It was not until the nineteenth century, however,
that English grammar was taught in British schools, and the secondary school I myself attended was (and still is) the Boston Public
Latin School.

The Latin grammar that was taught, however, was the grammar
of written Latin. No one knows how Latin was spoken, or even
how it was pronounced, for it ceased to be a living language almost
two millennia back. The chances are that it was every bit as messy
as present-day English, since the Romans must have been every
bit as lazy as we are. What they actually said when a Roman *he*
wished to convey the information that he loved a Roman *her* is lost
to us forever, but it is highly probable that he did not say "amo."

Few languages today retain all the inflections of Latin and
Greek, although the pedagogues have managed to maintain a
certain amount of pretense that they do. Thus in French the past
tense is almost uniformly carried by the presence of the vowel

sound that appears in the English word *gave*. The pretense of inflection is maintained by spelling it "ai" or "ait" or "ais" or "e," and since spelling exists only in the written language it can be said that inflection in that instance also exists only in the written language.

English of course finally became accepted as a language in its own right, and the pressure to teach English grammar in the schools became irresistible. Pedagogues, however, have their own way of fighting back. If they were to be forced to teach English, they would do so. But their dignity required that at least they be allowed to pretend it was Latin. And so they did, and so they do.

I should be fairer than that. Formal teaching of any kind requires some sort of codification. Some kind of order must be imposed upon a body of knowledge if it is to be efficiently conveyed. A living spoken language is by its very nature almost entirely arbitrary: I say "white house" to convey a certain item of information because everyone I know says "white house" for that purpose. If everyone I knew said "maison blanche" I would either say "maison blanche" or as a practical matter would be demonstrating a reluctance to communicate at all. If I chance to be in Quebec I can say either, as I may choose. There is no more to it than that.

What I say today, moreover, is in certain instances not what I would have said when I was younger. I learned—not in school but in my neighborhood—to say in certain circumstances "Whom did you give it to?" What I say now is "Who did you give it to?" What I was taught to say, and never have said, is "To whom did you give it?" I am fairly certain that my children, when they were children, were taught exactly the same.

I learned in my youth also to say "between him and me." I still do say "between him and me." I know perhaps a few dozen people, most of them my own age, who also say "between him and me." All the rest say "between he and I." I do not know what my sons say, but I am as sure as I am sure of anything that their children will say "between he and I." (When I write for television, by the way, every time I write "him and me" the next person to

get hold of the copy changes it to "he and I," and that is the way
it gets on the air. Quite right to do so, too.)

Irrelevant as it may be, I cannot resist adding that the current
usage requires "she gave it to him"; "she gave it to me"; and "she
gave it to he and I." It makes no sense at all to say that two of those
usages are "correct" and the third is "incorrect." All three are
entirely arbitrary, and are what they are. They are also all bad
Latin, but I do not speak Latin.

The pedagogues told me that I was entirely within my rights to
say "I will further protest" but might not under any circumstances
say "I intend to further protest." If I had asked the reason, I would
have been told that English grammar does not permit me to split
an infinitive, which is a lie. The real reason, as I noted earlier, was
that in Latin an infinitive is a single word and cannot be split;
whereas Latin did indeed tolerate auxiliary verbs, thereby legiti-
mizing slipping in an adverb here and there.

And so it went, and so it goes.

That burst of bad temper behind me, I should be able to get
back to the matter at hand, which is by no means an easy matter
to resolve. For all that I have said, it is undeniable that a writer
who lacks a firm command of English grammar is no writer at all.

A part of the problem has already been encountered in the
earlier discussion of spelling. Unless the grammatical construction,
in any given instance, is what the reader expects it to be, the whole
undertaking becomes what I might call fischy. It is not necessarily
that the item being read is incomprehensible; it is frequently quite
as comprehensible as the customary construction would have
been. But there has been a burst of noise in the system which is
disconcerting at the very least, and the reader's attention is likely
to be drawn to the noise rather than the signal; it is also likely to
arouse the suspicion that a writer who doesn't know how to say
something may quite possibly have nothing to say. The fact that
the suspicion is unwarranted becomes somewhat irrelevant, for
the damage is done.

I have abruptly shifted my attention from the spoken to the written word, where it belongs. The grammar of the spoken word underlies the grammar of the written word. But that relationship, complex enough when we speak of matters of vocabulary, becomes more complex still when grammar is under consideration just as the ordering of words is in some senses more complex and perhaps more important than the words themselves. Nowhere does the Bible suggest that "In the beginning was the sentence." In the evolution of language the sentence must have arrived quite late in the game. The written sentence arrived only yesterday.

I must go over old ground. However precise or even pedantic a speaker may be, his adherence to grammatical practices—I cannot bring myself to call them "rules"—is remarkably lax. Few speakers are unaware that a plural noun requires a plural verb form, but sound waves float in the air only momentarily and are quickly dissipated. Even the speaker may not recall whether the noun was singular—"the committee"—or plural—"the members." (The British, by the way, handle that particular example by decreeing that *committee* is a plural noun, which conveys some idea of why I call these matters practices rather than rules.) In the spoken language, none of this makes much difference, since the listener, too, is likely to have forgotten exactly how the statement began. More to the point, however, there are what might be called the auxiliary languages of tone and tempo and all the rest to help the listener extract meaning from the process, and with all that a lapse or two in grammar does not usually affect too profoundly the lucidity of the message.

The durability of the written word has significant consequences. The spoken word is in a process of constant flux; not one of us speaks as he spoke a decade back. We are always speaking the current spoken language, or pretty nearly. But as you read what I wrote ten years ago, you read exactly what I wrote then, and not what I would write today. It is clear as clear can be that anyone who would have written ten years ago "Burt Reynolds is a very gay man" would not for a moment dream of writing that sentence today, even though after a moment or two of shock it would confuse no one. Beyond that, the written language may very well fall into the hands of one who speaks a variant of the English in which it is written; an Australian, for example. It may even be read by one who speaks no English at all.

As a consequence of all this, the written language is managed extremely conservatively. There is no question that written language pursues the grammatical practices of the spoken language. But it pursues from far behind. It would be too much to say that cultivated writing reflects the cultivated speech of the second-last generation, but at least in some of its aspects it does so. (There are other aspects in which it reflects the speech of the second-last century, and still others in which it is not clear that it reflects any speech at all, although as a matter of faith I am certain it does.)

That conservatism is a social phenomenon, and like all such is the consequence of individual decisions or compulsions, for what a society tends to do is the sum of what all of its members tend to do, aggregated in fashions we do not quite understand. There is necessarily a period of transition during which there will be honest differences of opinion. In the end a few diehards cling to the old fashions and are consequently regarded as eccentrics even by their friends. None of that is to be deplored. It governs the pace of change, and keeps the language from a permanent state of flutter, which would be disconcerting to say the least.

Those who are by nature conservative about the written language, and even some who are not, are likely to become irascible. You will notice that I cling to the notion that the words *he* and *him* and so on differ in a fundamental respect from *she* and *her* and so on. The first group, as I see it and as the language has very nearly always seen it, refers either specifically to males or indifferently to males and females, as the context may suggest; the second exclusively to females. Clearly that usage is vanishing (along with all the silly words invented to fill what was conceived to be a gap). It is now considered necessary to write "he or she," "him and her."

But the old style will not entirely vanish, at least as long as I continue to speak and write. I might defend it by pointing out that of the two usages, mine alone is clearly <u>not</u> sexist, but I do not do so: it is a conservative view and nothing more, and its appeal is to tradition and nothing more.

In any case, written grammar cannot be picked up by simple exposure, by which I mean that kind of exposure that inescapably comes to all of us by virtue of being sentient and members of society. Written grammar must be mastered by some kind of learning process. It falls into no one's lap. Since we look upon educational institutions as our founts of learning, it is only reasonable that the task has fallen upon the pedagogue, and only reasonable that the pedagogue has desperately sought to codify the uncodifiable. That quite natural urge has led the pedagogue down strange trails, but it is easy to understand why.

Let me wander for a moment. As I implied a few pages back, five hours a week most weeks of the year were spent during my youth studying Latin. In no intelligent sense of the word did I actually learn Latin, and it would not have been particularly fruitful if I had, since no one I know reads Latin, or writes Latin, or speaks Latin. The labors I underwent did prove, however, to be enormously useful in helping me understand what my English teachers were saying when they spoke of "gerundives" and "conjugations" and "declensions" and "inflections." <u>Why</u> they were saying those things, unfortunately, I never did quite know, and do not really quite know now.

There is but a single way in which to learn the grammar of the written word: by reading the written word and writing it. And to learn it that way is a great deal more difficult than it sounds.

To begin with, good writing (and remember, I am dealing with expository writing) maximizes lucidity, delivering its message as clearly as the written language permits. As a consequence, it concentrates the reader's attention on the message and not on the manner in which it is delivered. (That sentence will later call for a chapter all its own.) The judicious adherence to grammatical practices will not be noticed; only the lapses will stand out, where by "lapse" I mean not a failure to abide by the "rules" but the presence of grammatical constructions that reduce lucidity. Reading for structure and not for content is extremely difficult, and the better the writer the more difficult it is.

There is, in fact, a great deal more to be gained from writing than from reading, provided always that the most important single aspect of writing is honored and heeded. *Writing is intended to be read.* It is intended in the first instance to be read by the person who wrote, who all the while seeks out ambiguity and obscurity and searches for exactly the grammatical construction that will reduce them or eliminate them. It is intended in the second instance to be read by others, who are prepared to say, "What on earth is that sentence supposed to mean?" and other kind words. In the instance of professional writers it is intended to be read sooner or later by an editor, who generally cannot himself write a lick and who may not be able to say with any clarity just what it is that constitutes good writing, but who damned well knows bad writing when he sees it.

The best English teacher is such an editor, creating for the student the only environment in which the written language can be learned: an environment in which error is exposed over and over again (which is also the environment in which the infant learns the spoken language). Fellow students, too, should be called into the process during the later years, for there is a double return for their investment: exposing the errors of their fellows, they learn of their own. Indeed, the enlistment of the students is probably inescapable, for the best educator in the world would blanch at the expenditure of time and energy necessary to deal simultaneously with several dozen writers.

Of all the tools available to the writer, grammar and syntax are the most essential, although not the most powerful, and the mastery of grammatical practices is a sine qua non. If a word is not understood, a good start can be made toward understanding, beginning with the short walk to a dictionary. There is no way at all to look up the meaning of a sentence, and the man who wrote it may be worst placed of all to puzzle out its meaning. It must be presumed that he <u>knew</u> what he intended to say when he wrote it, and he will find it most difficult to realize, on his own, that the sentence in question does not in fact clearly mean what he intended it to mean and indeed in extreme instances may very well mean nothing at all.

I trust I have eliminated any initial impression I may have conveyed that I have some kind of contempt for English grammar. It is the glue that holds together all the elements that constitute the language, written or spoken, but above all, written. I do not respect the manner in which it is generally taught, for a good many reasons. It is irrationally taught, but that does not matter to me nearly as much as the fact that the manner in which it is taught demonstrably does not work as it should. It may not even be too much to say that it does not work at all. What I am beginning to suggest may not be the best way, but it cannot be worse than what we have.

I have already written at some length about the value of the word processor as the writer's tool. It is clear that its ability to turn out hard copy, clean and neat and tidy, is almost an essential to the kind of teaching I have been adumbrating here, and of which I shall have considerably more to say.

These, then, are the tools. It remains to be seen how they are to be used to create expository writing. The interlude is over; we must get down to the hard work of thinking about writing itself.

Chapter Ten

What Am I Saying?

Of course you can play with them,
There's no harm in them.
They are only words. . . .

What? They've turned nasty?
They've clawed you and bitten you?
Dear me, there's blood all over the place,
And broken bones.
They were perfectly tame when I left them,
Something they ate must have disagreed with them.

You mean you fed them on *meaning?*
No wonder then.

    D. J. ENRIGHT

I PRESUME we have agreed that what we are dealing with, as we make our tortuous way forward, is a written document that seeks to deal with some nontrivial matter, and does so at some nontrivial length. I do not deny that there are examples of the written word that meet one of those criteria and not the other. A sign reading "BRIDGE OUT AHEAD" is brief but at the same time provides pressingly needed information; the autobiography of a film star is likely to be very long. As a good many billboards will reveal, quite short messages can be written with a great deal of craft, and no doubt there are books in which that craft is explored, but not here.

Each of the two criteria that I have chosen for expository writing makes a demand upon the writer. The first of the two signifies that he is setting out to say something. The question of just what he is setting out to say is thus laid on the table, and for the time being is the only one of the two criteria to concern him. For a long while it becomes moment by moment a more and more difficult question to answer.

I will invent a scenario, casting in the major role a writer, otherwise unspecified. At some moment of some day, under some circumstances, my writer says to himself or to a companion, "I shall write a book [or a dissertation, or a magazine article, or an essay for the Op-Ed page of the New York Times] on offshore fishing in Alaska." The very notion generates a glow of accomplishment, and encourages the writer to proceed immediately to the consideration of important related matters. I shall assume (after all, it is my scenario) that my writer is planning a book, rather than some other form of exposition. As a consequence, his first thoughts deal with the selection of a publisher, and he rapidly passes before his mind the names of those publishing houses which have at one time or another displayed an interest in fishing, or in Alaska, or in him. Having settled on a publisher, he then estimates the probable sales, generally settling upon 100,000 copies in hard cover, which should be worth about $200,000 for him, with paperbacks coming along later. Being a practical man, he appreciates the fact that sales of that magnitude are unlikely without a catchy title, and quickly settles upon Offshore Fishing in Alaska. With creativity still at the flood, he fixes upon the lady to whom the book will be dedicated. At that point or very near it, a feeling of completion, of a job well done, settles upon him, and he goes somewhere to get drunk.

The scenario should probably end right there, since most expository writing never gets written. But some of it does, and I shall continue, a bit more seriously.

As he thinks further about his book, the writer finds himself sketching out an outline in his head. The book must begin somewhere, but exactly where? Does he begin with an account of the various kinds of offshore fishing to be found in Alaska? Or perhaps with a reasoned argument for Alaska rather than the Virgin Islands? The history of Alaskan fishing? That might be better. And of course, "offshore" covers a lot of territory; perhaps he should define his subject more narrowly before going any further. Then there are the questions of fishing gear, and costs, and seasonal considerations. . . . And it must not be forgotten that planning a chapter on the history of fishing in Alaska is not quite the same as writing it, since he will have to find out just what that history is.

The writer, in short, has embarked upon his search for lucidity before he has written a single word. He is groping for the best possible structure for his document (I need that pallid word here) because that structure will have to carry the burden of all he plans to say. It must, to begin with, be the most logical structure he can design. But at the same time, it must be a compelling structure if it is a book intended for a wide audience, or a structure designed to emphasize what he is adding to knowledge of the subject if he is writing for a professional audience, or a careful step-by-step structure if it is to be a textbook or a manual.

And at just this point the second criterion comes into play. All that he has been thinking reinforces his initial impression that this is to be a reasonably long document, or if he did not begin with that impression, creates it. "Reasonably long" is vague; I mean it to be. The outline he is working out in his head will not fit in his head. It needs more work, and he can work on it efficiently only if he can hold it out at arm's length. In short, he needs it on paper. Before he can create the document he has in mind, he must create a document of another kind entirely: an outline.

I repeat, this is my scenario. I am not entirely certain how much of it is descriptive and how much prescriptive. For one thing, I am not acquainted with all the world's expository writers; for another, I have lumped together in the phrase "expository writing" a great many different kinds of documents.

I honestly believe that no writer, faced with a task that will require more than a few minutes of actual writing, sets out to write without an outline. There are times when the outline is rudimentary and held wholly in the mind. The journalist for a daily newspaper is at times obliged to work from that kind of outline, and the best of them perform miracles, considering the circumstances. But it is noticeable that the level of writing in a morning newspaper is higher than that in an evening newspaper simply because the reporter for the morning paper generally (but not always) has time to reflect before he sits down to write, and uses that time to plan what he will write; the P.M. journalist always has an imminent deadline to meet. (That was certainly so before the days of television; for all I know, firsthand, things may have changed, but it continues to seem true to me.)

It is also possible to let chronology provide the outline ready-made, and it might appear that autobiographies can be written so. But they would be lesser autobiographies, I am quite sure. Craftsmanship remains craftsmanship, and a strict chronology would be a straitjacket for anyone who had anything worthwhile to express.

Beyond that, at some point it becomes grossly inefficient and in the end impossible to hold an outline wholly in mind and to develop it wholly in mind. The young appear better equipped than the old for mental outline, but that may be for the most part illusory. It may be that advancing years bring a more critical attitude toward one's own work, and that the older writer is simply less likely to be satisfied with an outline he has not set down on paper. But of course, I myself happen to be an older writer, and perhaps it is to be expected that I should take that view.

It is in the written outline that paragraphs and under some circumstances chapters begin to take shape. Loosely speaking, an outline develops an argument, and the best of arguments proceed step by step. The large step is a chapter; a very large argument demands very many large steps. The paragraph is a short step; many short steps become equivalent to a large step. And the analogy is useful in one more respect: no step, large or small, ought to end with one foot in midair.

In all my life I have never been able to think of any more than that to say about a paragraph. It sets out to develop an item of thought: the smallest item of thought that can be distinguished from another item of thought. It continues until there is no more than can actually be said about that item of thought, and then stops. The pause after the paragraph is temporal when it is spoken, and represented by the waste of space in the written word. In the spoken word, it provides the opportunity for the speaker to examine the person or persons to whom he is speaking and judge whether that specific item of thought has in fact been communicated. If he believes it has not been, he repeats it another way. It provides also the opportunity for a listener to nod or to murmur "Uh-huh," to protect himself from having to hear it again.

Thinking, like walking, is a cumulative activity. One does not take first the first step and then the seventh; the intervening steps are intended to take the walker to where he can take the seventh. It is for that reason that a paragraph cannot be examined in isolation except in its technical conformation: trivially, are the words spelled right? less trivially, are the sentences lucid as sentences? It can be examined to ascertain whether the item of thought is most effectively set forth, but that examination must always take into account other paragraphs. More often than not, an unsound paragraph will be healed not internally but by adding or subtracting some other paragraph.

The function of the outline, then, is to mark out paragraphs and chapters and in extreme instances volumes. Beyond that, the form it takes will vary with the individual. An entry may be a single word if that suffices, or a long sentence, or several sentences. Quite frequently, it takes a form that is unintelligible to anyone but the author; if an extended period of time elapses between the preparation of the outline and the actual writing, it may very well be unintelligible to the author as well. Facing a cold outline can be a horrible experience; a prudent writer tends to create outlines which at the moment of creation he himself finds redundant.

Having created the outline, the writer abandons it.

Whether anyone who ever lived and wrote has managed to get an outline completely right is a question all its own. Indeed, the issue can be phrased even more strongly: Whether it is ever possible to get an outline completely right, in any but the most trivial instances, is no better than dubious. I myself have never known it to happen to me, and observation leads me to maintain that I have never known it to happen to others, but then I am acquainted with relatively few writers and I may have missed something.

There always appears to be room for improvement. I have already alluded to one kind of improvement. The outline is intended to prefigure a lucid document, but the outline itself is not necessarily lucid, or its lucidity may be transient. More than once I have encountered in an outline of my own a single word—a name, more often than not, but it can be anything at all—that must have reflected a headful of associations when it came to mind. The word remains in the outline; the associations have vanished. Staring at the word does not help a bit. Outlining is often done in what appears to be a burst of inspiration, and it takes real effort to slow the pace and leave a trail. Buried treasure is all very well, but not when there is no way to find it again.

That is a lesson that is learned by experience; the other defect of the outline is more fundamental. The writer, when he is engaged in shaping his outline, is in fact thinking very hard about what he plans to write. As my facetious scenario was meant to convey, the initial impulse to write is quite as likely to be based on fantasy as on any rational considerations, and the process really does not begin until the outline of a document, or some major portion of a document, begins to take shape. Now the writer is thinking, and if he is a responsible writer he is thinking hard.

Let me revert to offshore fishing in Alaska, and this time not facetiously at all. The very act of outlining such a book, if I were to undertake it as some kind of exercise, would almost immediately reveal to me that I was unable to write that book, or at least unable to write it in any reasonable period of time. I could not reasonably set down a pattern of paragraphs and chapters because the subtleties of the interconnections among paragraphs and chapters and the volume as a whole could not possibly be known to me until I was familiar with what the document as a whole was intended to say.

The case is extreme, since I have been fishing only four or five times in my life and my acquaintance with Alaska is limited to a few hours in Fairbanks during a blizzard. But in some degree, any outline will reveal to its creator alarming expanses of his own incapacity. Thinking hard about anything at all has the effect of laying bare vast areas of ignorance interspersed with an occasional isle of enlightenment. What is worse, the more a man knows about anything the more likely he is to be haunted by the depth of his own ignorance. (To be sure, I know some who seem to be immune to that phenomenon, but I don't like them.)

It must be obvious that I am merely skirting a more fundamental matter, which is whether it is ever possible to arrive at a point at which further thought is valueless. Is the mind infinitely productive? I don't believe that to be a question worth worrying about, one way or another, for a large variety of reasons, and I propose to give it no further thought, now or hereafter. As a practical matter, diminishing returns set in sooner or later, upon which (where the writer is concerned) the journalist's dictum takes effect: "Don't get it right; get it written!"

In short, sooner or later the writer must make do with the outline he has. The point at which that occurs depends upon many extraneous matters: his own temperament, his publisher's patience, possibly the state of his bank account.

The time always arrives when the writer must write. All in all, it is a pity. Until then, for any writer who does not write solely for money, it has been a pleasure. He has been extremely busy not writing a marvelous document (the pallid word is an offense in this context, but again I do not wish to be too specific), and although by this time he is aware that the document in the end will be flawed, as long as he continues not to write it the document remains marvelous. But now comes the hard work of doggedly putting down one word after another, day after day, perhaps week after week and month after month, and he knows that, try as he

may, they will not all be the right words in the right order. The
books we have in mind are all great books. And such fun, too! until
we have to write them.

What I have been describing is the process by means of which
the writer determines what he intends to say, and the manner in
which he will see to it that what he says is said as lucidly as may
lie within his power. He must now seat himself at his word processor, or his typewriter, or his lined yellow pad, and say it. He has
his outline for guide. And to some degree or another, the outline
crumbles in his hands.

That should not be surprising. To begin with, he cannot write
what he has to say without thinking of what he has to say, and the
act of thought will alter his perception of what he has to say. For
another, for the first time he is reading what he has to say; he is
interacting now not with his own central nervous system but with
an object that lies outside it. That very relationship is new, so far
as this particular project is concerned, and it is provocative, for
within certain limits he is hearing what he has to say as another
person might hear it. The outline created no such effect, any more
than examining the architect's drawing will tell a family how it will
feel to live in the house.

The degree of fidelity with which the document will resemble
the outline seems to me to be a matter of chance as far as my own
writing is concerned. I can recollect no occasion when there has
been a complete correspondence, and I do not believe it possible.
There has been at least one instance where there appears to have
been no correspondence at all. A half-completed book was simply
jettisoned and begun all over again because I had awakened in the
dead of night with the sudden recognition that there was a better
way to organize it, from first word to last.

I know also that the phenomenon is by no means limited to the
written word. The unique characteristic of expository writing is
that the outline of an extensive document and the document itself
are both in the same mode: the mode of the written word. The

outline of a motion picture or a television program or a play is also more often than not the written word—in any highly collaborative enterprise it almost must be—but the products are in another mode entirely. And in all those instances, it is most unusual when the product conforms closely to the outline.

I have made a distinction between what I chose to call "creative" and "expository" writing which for the moment I could do without. In the more customary usage of *creative* they are both acts of creation, as are films and most other kinds of communication. It may be that creativity, in that sense, cannot be turned on and off, and that it persists throughout the entire process, to the extent that a first-rate actor may be said to recreate his role each time he plays it. (I do not speak of drones; I do not speak anywhere in this book of drones. Well, maybe later.)

In any event, the document is ultimately completed (or abandoned altogether, which is none of our affair). In this account it began in fantasy, and I suspect that a good deal of writing begins that way, much of it being put away and forgotten somewhere along the line. In the more favorable instances it passes through a process of outlining and re-outlining until there appears to be no point in further outlines or no time to make them, and then through a further process in which it assumes its own shape, by no means independent of the outline but certainly not its slave. It achieves, finally, the status of a document: a book, an article, a report, possibly a long letter to the editor of the New York Times.

It would be absurd if you were to believe that it ends there, or should end there. Much remains. But let us leave it there for the moment, and reflect.

The time has come to circle back to where we were several thousand words back. I wrote then of the close association between writing and taking thought, and it was for that reason as much as anything else that I deplored the steady degeneration in writing skills. I want now to make the same point all over again, with considerably more force.

The process of writing an extensive document, as I have described it, is in every important respect the process we embark upon when we set out to think seriously of almost anything at all. Essentially we move repeatedly through some kind of argument, rearranging the line of thought, working over and over again through the rough spots, breaking the argument as a whole into its constituent parts and rearranging them so that the structure of the argument as a whole is clearly revealed and its weaker elements exposed, suspending the process from time to time because the raw material of the argument is deficient and a certain amount of study is required before the analysis can move forward. Every bit of that describes the solitary thinker quite as nearly as the solitary writer.

No one is likely to be surprised by the statement that writing, or at least the kind of writing I am dealing with, cannot be managed without thinking. I am not quite prepared to argue that the kind of thinking I am considering can be managed without writing. But I teeter on the edge of some such claim.

Writing, as I have said, creates an object, with all the benefits that accrue. It can be studied as intensely as one might wish by the man who wrote it and the men who read it. A vagrant notion passing through the mind, however powerful that mind may be, cannot.

The vagrant notion, and even the settled notion, are deficient in other serious ways as well. They lull. As often as not, they provide an illusion of work that has been done, and even well done, while all the while the real work has not so much as been initiated. "At this point," says the thinker, "I will show that tall men suffer lower back pains more frequently than short men," and goes on contentedly with his mental labors. He has shown nothing of the sort. Indeed, he has not even <u>said</u> (unvoiced) what he means with any degree of clarity. But he may very well go forward under the illusion that he is progressing with admirable alacrity toward his goal, whatever that might be.

For exactly that reason, a most alarming proportion of all the essays and books that are undertaken are almost at once abandoned. (I don't really know why I call it alarming.) Once the act of writing begins, and the epistle dedicatory has been neatly wrapped up, the author realizes for the first time that the product so tidily and attractively packaged in his mind is mirage and nothing more, and vanishes the moment he comes close to it. Then, abruptly, he becomes aware of the labors that must be performed before he will have anything that appears to be a manuscript. And at that moment, usually, he goes out and plays tennis. E. B. White once wrote a jingle with the refrain:

Sing ho, sing hey, sing ho, sing hey,
He thinks he'd like to write a play,
But only at certain times of day

which pretty much says it, although it is not plays we have in mind.

The identification of writing with thinking, and of thinking with writing, seems even to have become built into the common tongue. In ordinary speech an author rarely says, "That is what I wrote," unless he wishes to emphasize the fact of publication rather than the substance; we will more often say, "That is what I said." Indeed, I sit here writing, but the chapter upon which I am currently engaged is called "What Am I Saying?" The process that occupies me, and which I am discussing, is only secondarily a process of writing.

If all this is accepted, it carries along with it certain implications which may very well be disturbing. To a very large degree, the pedagogical approach to writing looks upon it as something very much like a mechanical act, not significantly different from the act of adding long columns of figures. One learns how it is performed, and thereafter performs it habitually. The fact that seven plus four equals eleven is not something we are obliged to think about; it has become hard-wired into the mind (if I may employ the useful jargon of the times) and whatever effort it ever involved went into making the connections.

The antipathy most people have toward the very idea of "artificial intelligence," whatever else it may mean, marks a certain repugnance toward the idea that thinking can be looked upon as a purely mechanical activity. We seem to be quite willing to concede that some folks think more efficiently than other folks (always placing ourselves among the "some" rather than the "other"). We seem also to be able to live quite comfortably with the realization that there is little, or perhaps nothing, that can be done about it except at the margins, where the hard fact is that it does not do much good.

In this roundabout way, I am asserting that only some members of society, and not all, are capable of doing the kind of writing that is being discussed here. That assertion is swathed in ignorance. I do not know how many makes "some": 5 percent or 15 percent or 50 percent. I think it is closer to 15 percent than either of the other two figures, but if I am asked for evidence I can only mumble. (I also think that I am among the "some" rather than the "other," but I really cannot make a very good case for that, either.)

What seems to make me odd man out is that I am not terribly bothered by the state of affairs I describe. Indeed, I find it extremely satisfactory that some people do some things and other people do other things, and I quite definitely believe that the horror of a society in which everyone specialized in taking thought was what led the good Lord to haul down the Tower of Babel.

So far as "writing skills" are concerned, I would wish to see the educational system recognize at least this disparity among those it serves. I sincerely believe it to be within the capacity of the system to help those who write well to write better, just as I believe the system can help those who think well to think better; obviously I believe the two go together. I think that those who believe (whether they know it or not) that writing is a mechanical skill are distorting the educational system, in part so that they may be at peace with their own deceit, and that they do real damage.

I leave the matter there for the moment, as an unsupported opinion. You may be sure I will come back to it.

Shall I confess it? I must now go back to my outline.

Chapter Eleven

To Whom?

> The author is like the host at a party. It is
> his party, but he must not enjoy himself so
> much that he neglects his guests. His
> enjoyment is not so much his own but theirs.
>
> CHARLES P. CURTIS, A Commonplace Book

THEN there is the audience to consider. It is not the straightforward problem that it might appear. Not infrequently there will be several audiences, which causes a certain kind of problem. But that problem cannot be tackled satisfactorily until the problem of the initial audience—the audience that holds pride of place—is resolved. That audience, as you may very well have guessed, is the writer himself.

Once the notion is accepted that writing is a process of objectifying the act of taking thought, it becomes obvious that in the early stages of the process the writer must be his own prime audience. That is the case almost beyond qualification during the period in which an outline is being perfected, as long as the writer continues to possess the time and the patience for outlining. During that period, the writer is confidently dividing the subject matter with which he intends to deal into two categories: those aspects he can take for granted; those of which he is not yet quite certain. The confidence may be misplaced, but he has a chicken and egg problem: he cannot create a satisfactory outline until he knows what he has to say; he cannot be reasonably certain just what he has to say until he has an outline fairly well in hand.

The portion he can take for granted goes very nearly unrepresented in the early stages of the outline, and at the extreme may go unrepresented entirely. At the extreme, of course, it will appear trivial, largely because it is trivial. The writer makes the basic assumption that he knows the meaning of the words and phrases he uses, even though they may be exceedingly cryptic, and he may be aware that no one else in the whole wide world can comprehend them quite as he does. When my outline carries the words "Popper quotation," only I know, at that moment, exactly which quotation from the extensive works of Karl Popper I have in mind.

And as I have noted, even I may not know, although when I set the words down I am firmly convinced that I do. Alive as the two words *Karl Popper* may be when I set them down, they may very well die with the passage of time, for over the years I have read a good deal of Popper and remembered a fair amount. The man does not live who has not pulled from his pocket, at one time or another, a crumpled sheet of paper upon which he wrote four or five words he now finds completely incomprehensible. They were important enough to write down, at some moment or another; in a week or a day or even a few hours they have become gibberish.

But the problem persists even when the outline is being converted into a finished manuscript. Indeed, it intensifies, because it appears in more complex forms, just as the manuscript itself is more complex than the outline upon which it is constructed.

I have been using, quite artlessly, the word *audience* to refer to the reader or the readers. It is the customary word, and it would be a mistake to scramble for a substitute. But *audience* carries powerful connotations of listening rather than of reading. It is fair enough; as I have emphasized, almost all of us do "listen" when we read or write. Yet we do not always hear the same sounds, although we read the same words.

I dealt earlier, and quite briefly, with the uses of incongruity, and in an earlier draft of this manuscript had written, "It is a positive distraction, which at its best adds to the sharpness of the writing." In that sentence (which you will no longer find where it once appeared) I intended *positive* to connote "welcome" or "useful," just as we discriminate (unless we are careful to avoid clichés) between "positive" and "negative" criticism. But positive has another meaning: it is used as an intensifier, as when we say, "He is a positive idiot."

With that awareness in the forefront of your mind, you may <u>hear</u> the word *positive* quite differently in the two sentences "It is a *positive* distraction" and "He is a *positive* idiot." Indeed, you can <u>say</u>, "It is a positive distraction," in two quite different ways, and thereby give it either of two distinct meanings and indeed two quite opposite significations. When I wrote the manuscript I knew beyond any trace of uncertainty just what I intended, and invariably read it in a manner appropriate to my intention. As a consequence, I never did realize that it was miserably phrased. Another reader, who did not labor under the disadvantages of my own assurance, underlined *positive* and put a large, vulgar exclamation point in the margin.

As in the instance of the cryptic outline, the writer himself may be first to be affected. Samuel Pepys must more than once have looked back in his diary and said to himself, "What could I have meant by that?" Sooner or later, the sound of the voiced sentence may be lost to memory, and the ambiguity of the written sentence thrusts itself forward upon the very man who wrote it.

That example is clear, although the point itself is fairly subtle. More frequently the problem arises with the writer's own vocabulary. Since every man's vocabulary is unique, and since it is so much a part of him that he has no way of knowing exactly how it is unique, he will inevitably use words and phrases which carry meanings with which others are not entirely familiar, or connotations which are entirely private. The vocabulary, however, will change with time. Here the richness of the passive vocabulary comes into play. There are words I used at one time of my life with a casual familiarity but which I use no more, although I need not be aware of it. Those words, however, are still in my passive vocabulary, and the casual familiarity remains when I encounter them in another's prose, or after the passage of time even in my own.

The Pepyses among us are not numerous. Most of those who write do so in the expectation that there will be other readers—one other, when the document is a personal letter, and millions of others at those moments when fantasy is given free play. "To whom?" then becomes a matter of prime importance.

Quite obviously, the mass audience is an undifferentiated audience. There is little that all members of such an audience will have in common, and what little there is will be somewhat primitive. Dickens expected tears when he wrote of the death of Little Nell, and was himself tearful as he wrote it, for little will more reliably draw tears than the account of the death of an innocent maiden. An innocent lad is not nearly as good a bet, I am not sure why. And let me add that I am not by any means sneering, for I am a member of that undifferentiated audience, and no doubt you as well, although for all I know you may well be one of those who deny they watch television.

But it was Dickens I chose to cite, for writing for an undifferentiated audience almost invariably suggests what I have been calling *creative writing*. My own biases are such that I cannot really envisage careful description and serious argument directed toward an undifferentiated audience except under most unusual circumstances, although there are books that make the pretense of doing just that and they are to be found each week in the best-seller lists. Those books—once more leaving aside the exceptional circumstances—I somewhat cavalierly take to be creative writing, for what they appear to do is make fiction out of fact, as unobtrusively as their authors can manage. It is not surprising that books dealing with diet, with sexual activities, with avarice and with quasi-religious urges predominate. (In this context, "diet" and "sexual activities" are closely connected.) All those matters make their homes far down the brain stem.

Exceptional circumstances arise when the expository writers are entitled to be considered artists rather than craftsmen, which is my own way of saying that I am not able to deal with them. Instances do not come easily to hand, exactly as one would expect. I would happily cite the translators of the King James Bible among the ancients, but among the moderns citations are more arguable: one man might bring forward Lewis Thomas and another John Kenneth Galbraith, but either would raise hoots in certain circles. Art is generally stimulated by a powerful urge to create, and it is not surprising that those writers who have written with great art for the mass audience have been creative and not expository writers. The names are not quite legion, but they do make a respectable list.

The problems which should concern us are the problems that arise with the differentiated audience, and most expository writing is directed to such audiences. They are not necessarily small audiences. The New York Times audience is quite differentiated, and not what any writer would be likely to call small if he were to write a book which reached that audience in its entirety.

But audiences may be quite small, and expository writing is in fact predominantly directed toward those quite small audiences. In some senses, moreover, that is by far the most important expository writing that is being done, and it is being done day by day by the largest number of individuals, few of whom look upon themselves as writers. To that extent it constitutes one of the most pressing and the most demanding problems now faced by the educational system, and we must deal with it here at length.

In very broad general terms, I speak here of the midrank staff assistant to a not particularly eminent member of the United States House of Representatives. His communication with the man he serves is likely to be almost exclusively in the form of "staff papers"—written memoranda and reports, both of which constitute expository writing in its purest form. What is more, although it is probable that the not particularly eminent member of the House of Representatives knows a good deal about winning elections, it is equally probable that everything else he knows will come from those staff papers, which (since he is a busy man) may be all that stand between him and total ignorance of what he is expected to do, once elected. I exaggerate, but not much. Possibly I do not exaggerate.

A staff paper will have been written with the congressman in mind, but if it survives scrutiny a good many other people will read it and modify it. Since I postulated the writer to be a midlevel member of the staff, it will be read by those who supervise and share his responsibilities before it reaches the congressman, possibly by members of the staff of other members of the relevant subcommittee, and more rarely by those members themselves; it will be cannibalized for use in other staff papers; and fragments of it may appear in the subcommittee's report. If the matter with which it is concerned is more than parochial, the staff paper will at one time or another be leaked to, or purloined by, a journalist from the Washington Post or even the New York Times. At the extreme, it will reach the hands of a writer for a major network news service, who will reduce it to thirty seconds of reading time and otherwise make it fit provender for an anchorman. In all, as many as fifteen or twenty readers will give it some measure of attention. And the consequence of all that attention may be almost anything you might imagine, from an increment of a few million dollars in the national debt to nuclear war.

What I have just described goes on hour after hour, day after day, almost wherever there are men at work. Gordon Thompson, who is something of an authority on such matters, has estimated that "half the working population of America is now engaged in pushing pieces of information about." They are not all staff papers or the equivalent: some are raw information, such as balance sheets and inventories. But that raw information comes into existence largely to provide the substance of those papers.

It is not too much to say that expository writing directed to one

kind of differentiated audience or another has become the heart
of the process in which what people know and think is converted
into what people do. It was not always so; indeed, as it now exists
it is a phenomenon of the twentieth century. But its roots go back
to the invention of the alphabet, triggering the explosion of knowledge and culture in ancient Greece, and subsequently to the invention of movable type and that other explosion known as the
Renaissance. It may well be that we are in the midst of a third such
event, brought about by the computer or, more generally, the
transistor, but we will not be sure of that until the twenty-first
century rolls around, if it does.

The differentiated audiences with which I have been dealing—
pockets of ten or thirty or a hundred readers, many of whom are
also collaborators—are the targets of very nearly all the expository
writing that is produced in this or any other advanced country.
There are other and larger differentiated audiences for which
newspaper articles and books and magazines are published.
(There is also a cascading effect to which I have alluded but which
I will not consider beyond this parenthesis: the writer for television news or documentaries addresses directly his colleagues, and
through a few of those colleagues an extremely large differentiated audience, although not nearly as large an audience as that
addressed by those who write situation comedies.)

The distinction can be made, loosely enough, in another way.
Some reading is done at home, some at the office. A great many
people, and almost all those who influence the course of events in
any substantial way, do most of their reading at the office. And
most writing is done by just those people and not by the journalists
or the academics, who are the other principal producers of expository prose.

Addressing such an audience imposes special obligations on the
writer. He must be aware of his audience with every word he
writes. To the extent that his audience has its own vocabulary, he
must be at home with it. To the extent that it has its own syntactical habits, or grammatical preferences, or even typographical ar-

rangements, he must be aware of them. He need not conform to them absolutely; indeed, he must not, since it may very well be a part of his task to alter them. (One of my own few proud moments arrived when something I had written persuaded a group of strong-minded individuals to alter their own usage of the words *educational television* to mine.)

Under those circumstances, the writer is engaged in a balancing act. If he is to maximize lucidity, he must create for his immediate purposes an active vocabulary that can be found within the passive vocabularies of all those within the differentiated audience he addresses (which is not difficult when the audience is as small as those we are now considering) and that satisfies their preferences (which is somewhat more difficult). He departs from that vocabulary only at some risk. To be sure, it is a risk he must take when his judgment tells him so, but risks of that sort should never be taken in ignorance. He will have similar obligations with respect to syntax and idiom, but within a small audience those are usually well codified and cause little difficulty.

I am not proposing that a writer do violence to the language he writes, in the name of momentary conformity. For reasons I find obscure, certain groups of academics, most of them economists, have lately taken to saying and writing such phrases as "Absent an efficient market . . . " I shall continue to write "In the absence of an efficient market . . . " thus marking myself no member of the group. Doing so, I lose status but not lucidity; that, at least, is the judgment I have made. But as I have noted, writing for an audience of linguists I am obliged to use such words as *phoneme* and *morpheme* because I otherwise lose lucidity. More subtly, writing for an audience of physicists I must be careful in my metaphorical employment of such words as *momentum,* for the word has for physicists a life of its own which argues against its loose employment in metaphor.

I have been leading to a stronger statement than those I have been making. The question of "to whom" is being considered here after a long chapter on "what." For the writer, it comes first. It is a prior consideration, for more often than not it affects his planning long before he begins to consider exactly what he will say, and it must be completely resolved before he begins to say it.

Consequences follow which are not immediately obvious. Accustoming himself to think of his task in that fashion, the writer has company in the room as he goes about it. The audience is always present in his mind, and their presence can confer a kind of animation upon what he is doing as much as it confers a direction. If there is a single remark about the writer's craft that can be made without qualification, it is that writing is a lonely way to spend one's time. Hours of association with even a word processor are not enlivening. The awareness of an audience helps.

The manner in which the craft of expository writing is generally taught when it is taught at all, at the lower levels of education and more often than not the higher levels as well, rarely takes account of the audience or does so only in an abstract way. The loneliness is stressed, the company ignored. In most instances the student is obliged to assume that the instructor is the sole member of his audience, and is likely to judge quite justifiably that he, or more probably she, is not a particularly interested audience.

Some years ago I was obliged to look into the question of courses in remedial writing at colleges and universities. I uncovered over a period of a few months one such program which was clearly making progress. It was remedial education at an extremely high level, I must admit, being provided for the very able students in the Kennedy School of Government at Harvard University (and it is shocking that remedial writing courses should be found necessary at all for such students). In that course, each assignment was accompanied with a specification of the person or persons to whom the document was to be addressed and the accompanying circumstances. Writing, in short, was taught as it is in fact performed. The instructors were persuaded that the effect of that technique was immediate and apparent; so was I. But it remains the exception and not the rule.

I have threatened that this book will become progressively

more pedagogical as it proceeds, and I am beginning to make good that threat. If, as I maintain, expository writing is an essential part of the process of taking thought, and if there is a confidence that thinking clearly and efficiently is itself of surpassing importance, then an educational system that cannot or does not effectively teach the craft of expository writing is as seriously deficient as an educational system can be. I am not appealing for some undefined "excellence in education," for as I have already maintained, such an appeal can be nothing but cant. The present educational system delivers to the country's most selective and most eminent universities not only students who are in need of remedial writing courses but faculty who are in general no better off. (I do not allude to the English faculty, but neither do I exclude it entirely.) It is not too much to say that such a state of affairs calls for attention.

In all good conscience I cannot leave the matter there. The document prepared for twenty pairs of eyes, more or less, is the kind of document in which I am most interested, but at this very moment I myself am engaged in writing a document prepared for a good many more eyes than that, and I cannot very well assume the attitude that the very small audience is the only audience worth our attention.

Any reading audience, however large, remains a differentiated audience if the document in question is much longer than four words or so. To be dismissive about even such tiny documents is slightly cavalier, since advertising men devote days and weeks to the formulation of such sentences as "Winston tastes good like a cigarette should" or that sparkling gem of earlier years, "99 44/100ths % Pure." They are able to compose at the rate of no more than one word in several days simply because their audience is *not* differentiated, which makes communication with it considerably more difficult. But writing advertising copy is not something about which I have anything much to say, although I have put in my time.

Go much beyond the slogan and those bits of writing that enjoin the citizen to keep off the grass or direct him to Track, or Gate, 14, and in terms of the number of those who are formally literate even the mass audience for the written word is quite small. Some quite significant proportion of the population does not read a book from one year to the next, and indeed may not so much as pick up a book except perhaps to throw. There is no practical way to find out how large that proportion is, since those are few who will admit they are a part of it. Even the great mass magazines of a few years back appealed to a relative few. Life, even though it devoted more attention to pictures than to prose and was virtually given away, circulated among about 5 percent of the literate public, although by means of hokery-pokery it was able to convince itself and a few others that as many as 15 percent or so read it. The real number may have been closer to 3 percent, which was remarkable enough.

Very probably, the proportion of the literate who read expository prose in gulps larger than a half dozen words or so was far larger in the past than it is today. A long way back, when few could read, those few in all likelihood read a good deal. Some kind of maximum, in terms of the population as a whole, may have been reached sometime during the first third of this century simply because the literate then constituted a substantial part of the population, and a few moments at a hand-held calculator will persuade you that 10 percent of 90 percent comes out to a good deal more than 50 percent of 10 percent. First radio and then television changed all that.

I threatened digressions, but all this is not entirely beside the point. Considering only the mass audience, it is clear there is far more communication than ever before in history addressed to, and received by, audiences en masse. In the terms with which we began, some 55 percent of all Americans are exposed each evening to description and argument through the medium of the network news broadcasts. At that level, such an audience can reasonably be called undifferentiated. But those who do the writing that precedes those telecasts—and except in rare instances the writing does come first—in practice are writing for the highly differentiated and quite small audience comprising their colleagues, their employers, and a handful of advertising agencies. Taken all together, in all its aspects (of which the sheer size of the ultimate audience is not the least important), that constitutes a social phenomenon without parallel in the past, and what it signifies no man can say. I now abandon the whole subject, reluctantly, although it may very well be that I shall get back to it one day.

The large audiences that the expository writer is likely to address are in absolute terms not large at all. Nothing could be more concrete an example than what I am doing right now, here at my desk. I am addressing an audience that is numbered at most in the tens of thousands. In moments of low spirits, I am aware that my audience may in fact turn out to be a few dozen or so: the friends and acquaintances who are good enough to read the manuscript, and several publishers who decline to publish it. There is one manuscript of that sort—but only one, I am happy to say—on the bookshelves behind me. In moments of extremely high spirits, I envision an audience of 100,000 or so. But such moments are rare and pass rapidly, although there is one such book, mostly but not entirely my own—but only one, I am unhappy to say—on the bookshelves behind me. Most of the time I think quite contentedly of 10,000 or so, and I have several of those.

That audience of 10,000 or so has been on my mind since I first began to consider writing this book and not another book or no book at all (which is known these days as "a viable option"). So far as what I am writing is concerned, the difference between 10,000 and 100,000 is not significant, although in other aspects, such as the amounts carried by subsequent Form 1040s, it may be significant indeed.

If, however, I had sat me down to write a book on the written word directed toward an audience of 1,000,000, I would be writing a different book entirely. I would begin by trying to fix in my mind the nature of that audience of one million, and my immediate conclusion would be that no such audience exists for serious description and argument dealing with the written word. (I will qualify that sentence shortly.) Having reached that conclusion, I will consider the matter further only if I am prepared to cease practicing my trade, which is expository writing, and become a creative writer instead. Since I like what I now do, and since I don't really need the money, and since I do not have the best of track records as a creative writer, the conclusion is pretty much foregone.

Still . . .

I might decide to try. If I did, the central theme of all I am in fact now writing would become irrelevant. Thinking now of my audience, I would no longer be struggling to be as lucid as my skills and my general capacity and the nature of the language permit me to be, but to simulate lucidity in a fashion that will deceive that audience into believing I am writing expository prose, which is another trade entirely.

I must insist that I have no objection to simulation per se. It lies at the heart of all creative writing, whether it is exemplified in Hamlet or in the works of Agatha Christie, and when it is done by a creative artist it is the noblest of all the uses of the written word, and a skill I would give everything I own to possess. But I do object to the simulation of expository writing, and I would propose that those who consciously perform it be paid in simulated money.

I can make the distinction by restating an earlier point. In true expository writing, the writer himself is part of the audience: he is thinking through what he is writing as he writes it. In simulated expository writing he is merely pretending to be part of the audience; he is concerned primarily and perhaps only with how he is writing. I cannot deny he is a craftsman, but it is a craft I find neither interesting nor admirable. Well, as the essayist said several hundred years back, "It is myself I portray."

A qualification was promised a few lines back, and will now be entered. There is a form of expository writing that has so far been neglected, and that may seem inconsistent with a few of the verities I have been expounding. I have in mind the textbook written for use at the secondary-school level or above. Nowhere is the struggle for lucidity more fiercely waged, since nowhere is the need for lucidity more desperately felt. But the textbook that sells 100,000 copies is by no means a rarity, and authors have been known to become indecently wealthy.

They represent instances of an odd kind of multiple audience. One is a small and highly differentiated audience which makes decisions to employ or not to employ the book in question; the other the large and not necessarily well differentiated audience served by the textbook. There is, in short, an important and sizable intermediate audience to which the writer must refer if he is ever to meet the ultimate audience.

The writer who satisfies both those audiences is the writer who becomes wealthy. At the university level at least he has earned all he gets. Such books as Paul Samuelson's introductory economics text are masterpieces of expository writing. At the secondary-school level the decision to purchase is made in another kind of shop, but even so a few first-rate texts slip through, although it is less likely in civics or English literature or history, where every God-fearing citizen is a self-appointed expert, than in physics or mathematics or geography.

There was a brief period during which paperback books were plentiful and seemed inexpensive, and as a consequence works intended as straightforward expository writing were adopted as texts at the undergraduate level. They do not appear inexpensive any longer, although measured against the cost of tuition they are probably no more costly than they used to be. While they lasted, they served the abler students better than explicit textbooks.

Whatever their destination, textbooks are a special case. We need consider them no further.

The threat of solipsism is behind us, or at worst off to one side, for the honest writer in some degree remains a solipsist a good deal of the time. I have said that the writer's vocabulary is in an important sense unique, and I shall be saying soon that his style, at bottom, is also unique. What he writes, however, he shares with others, and they are present as he writes. His universe, after all, is populated by more than his own paltry self.

Chapter Twelve

Why?

No man but a blockhead ever wrote
except for money.

SAMUEL JOHNSON

A SHORT CHAPTER, not because there is so little to say but because so much is inextricably intertwined with other aspects of the written word, and consequently has appeared in earlier pages.

Writing, when it is practiced over periods longer than a few minutes, is not carried to completion without a certain amount of discomfort. Without the benefit of the word processor, it is wearing and tedious, and even with the word processor it is more than a little of both. Few writers would say otherwise and mean it. As a result, a good deal of writing never happens, which is to be deplored, or possibly not.

Most writers of my acquaintance find it useful if not essential to establish some kind of pattern within which their writing is done. Once the pattern takes hold, that old devil habit puts in an appearance. Write from 9 A.M. to noon, keep it up for a week or so, and a fair amount of discomfort will set in on the morning you fail to write, even if that morning is spent in activities closely related to writing. I dare say that much the same would happen if you were to beat your head against a brick wall for three hours a day, a method of passing time to which writing upon occasion appears quite similar.

Georges Simenon, a most prolific novelist and as skilled as he was prolific, carried pattern-making to a point where it can only be called self-hypnosis. Each time he began a novel, he established a pattern that determined all that he did during the days that followed: the hours during which he wrote, and ate, and strolled, and listened to music, and slept. More than that, each meal on each day was precisely the meal he had eaten on the first day; each stroll covered exactly the same ground; even the music had to be the work of the same composer. As an ordinary matter, he wrote each of his novels a chapter a day for eleven days, after which he broke the pattern as ruthlessly as he had established it and did no writing at all for six weeks or so.

Somerset Maugham, after a good many decades, had so established his own pattern that he proved unable to break it at all. He lived a long life, and ultimately his skills departed, but thereafter until very nearly the day of his death he wrote short stories about which he had no illusions. They were not worth publishing, and Maugham knew it, but he went right on writing.

I chose to illustrate my point with two creative writers. Far more than the expository writer they can do without extensive reference to anything more than their own fancy and their general experience; they are not stopped short by something they simply do not know or had not anticipated. But the expository writer makes the same use of pattern, and to some degree becomes a slave to his pattern.

Even after the pattern is established, however, there is likely to be a significant interval between the moment when he is seated at his desk and is absolutely, unarguably, and most efficiently prepared to begin writing, and the subsequent moment when he actually begins writing. In the interval he may make an unnecessary telephone call or two, or empty all the ashtrays. In other days, when I did much of my writing in my office, I employed the time to sharpen pencils, despite the fact that my secretary had already checked to see that my pencils were sharp (I sharpened them anyway) and despite the somewhat more surprising fact that I had abandoned once and for all the use of pencils when I discovered ballpoint pens.

A more subtle prior problem, however, is frequently encountered. The experienced writer of expository prose knows exactly what he is in for once the pattern is established, and finds himself reluctant to establish the pattern in the first place. That reluctance may signify that whether he knows it or not he is really not ready to begin writing, simply because he still lacks sufficient command of his material, whatever it may be. Since I include the preparation of a written outline within *writing,* a reluctance of that kind is beneficial, for it is labor-saving.

None of this is idle chatter. The reluctance, in any form, is natural enough. But what is generally called "writer's block" is either a useful warning or an excuse. The experienced writer will generally recognize it as such when it really is a warning, and do what he must do to become ready to write. But even in that case, the experienced writer who also faces a deadline will grimly establish the pattern, though he may be aware that much he writes while the pattern is taking hold must later be jettisoned, and that what he finally is willing or obliged to let pass as finished product will never be all it should be.

The prospect of really writing, as distinct from wanting to write, or hoping to write, or simply intending to write, is grim. No one is likely to embark upon it without some reason, and there are a good many to choose from.

One reason is of course compulsion, which takes two quite distinct forms. The educational system obliges all of us to write as long as we are within it, unless we happen to begin our education in some kind of system which equates radical reform with mindless reform. The compulsion is not nearly as insistent as it used to be, but it is still there. If nothing more than the mechanical aspects of *writing* are taken into consideration, even the dyslexic has his problems mostly solved, and everyone learns. Those who are not called upon to write after they leave school, in the sense of the word as we have been considering it, promptly forget whatever they may have learned, and why not?

The writing that takes place under educational compulsion is often, and perhaps predominantly, to be classified as "creative writing." Much needs saying about that, but for the present I shall continue to use *writing* as a short form for *expository writing,* which by this time should cause no trouble. The warning is prudent, since if that usage is not kept in mind a good deal of what follows will appear to be clearly rubbish.

Another kind of compulsion is a consequence of employment. In more and more occupations with the passage of every year, advancement carries with it the obligation to absorb and transfer information, and much of that obligation must be met through the medium of the written word. It is useful, moreover, to discriminate further, in a somewhat different and less easily specifiable fashion, between what might be called "willing" and "unwilling" writers-under-compulsion. What is more, I shall insist on treating the difference as being fundamentally temperamental, assuming merely that some people are willing and some are not, and leaving the matter there. By doing so, I create a very large category of men and women who are obliged to write, and do so, but who sincerely wish they did not have to.

The make-up of that category is every bit as varied as one might wish. It includes an extremely high percentage of those who hold tenure in colleges and universities; most executives and upper-level managers of whatever enterprise you might choose to mention; much of the staff of the legislative, executive and judicial branches of government at all levels; a fair percentage of those who handle the routine correspondence of enterprises of any sort; in short, not all but certainly most of those who make the twentieth-century world wag. All in all, important people. Writing is a substantial part of how they make their living. And because they do it unwillingly, they are likely to do it badly.

Indeed, that category is large enough to permit me the assertion that most people write for money. In its own way, that is rather heartening. As Senator Dole said of the vice-presidency, it is nice inside work with no heavy lifting: It is accordingly a good deal more consonant with human dignity than shoveling slag, which is what a great many people did once upon a time. Then, too, few people are naturally mischievous, so it is fair to say that most of that writing is well meant.

One might suggest still another category, made up of those who write under compulsion but do so willingly. The words thus on display constitute a remarkably clear instance of the fashion in which pure logic and sound language can combine to create utter nonsense. Best consider them no further.

Clearly, those who write willingly are likely to be temperamentally attracted to employment in which writing is involved. Journalism still attracts a great many such people, but the meaning of the word has changed over the past few decades until it is not entirely safe to assume any longer that a journalist writes or even reads. I am being harsher than need be: as a matter of fact, most of them can read.

It is my impression, and nothing more, that most such men and women begin writing quite young, but come rather late to expository writing, by which I mean during their years of secondary-school education or considerably later. The shift from creative writing to expository writing often comes after a lapse of time in which very little extensive writing at all is attempted. I have no battery of data with which to buttress my case; it reflects a certain amount of casual observation and nothing more.

In all likelihood, the conversion is the consequence of a personal maturation, which arrives at different periods of their lives for different people. The maturation, in this instance, represents the development of a critical attitude toward one's own writing. Once such an attitude develops, an enormously large proportion of those who set out to be creative writers, whether as a pastime or with more or less vague notions of a career, are obliged to confront the fact that they do not have the talent for creative writing, or to put it more bluntly, that their short stories, essays, novels or plays, coldly considered, are abominable. That this should occur is not at all surprising, for the talent to produce even second- or third-rate creative writing is extremely rare. Then, too, talent or no talent, the learning period is often quite long, and no doubt many who have latent talent become discouraged as the rejection slips accumulate.

The educational system, from beginning to end, is such as to conceal or to deny these aspects of writing, obvious as they are. As quickly as the child is able to form letters he is encouraged to write "stories" and "plays," and praised for the lamentable scribblings that are the consequence. I suspect that a vicious circle emerges: the individual as a child is encouraged to think of himself as a creative writer, discovers at eighteen or twenty or twenty-five that he is nothing of the kind, and with little else in his education that is of any value or that suits his temperament, returns to the educational system bent on teaching others to be creative writers.

I have before me the newsletter of a national educational institution which I think may be the largest and best-supported "writing project" in the country. The project itself is directed toward secondary-school students, and the newsletter is intended to assist their teachers. The issue in question includes a lengthy article entitled "Teaching Poetry Writing with Computers." I shall forbear comment on the notion itself and simply quote a few of the "poems." (The article reports that the authors "range from fourth grader to university professor.")

The words
    masterful, serving
for inspiration
    gently, insistently
solace.

The riveter
Brawny, sweatcaked at Miller Time
Carefully slouches
Bethlehembound.

The reptilian brain
     sweet, juicy
in the nick of time's swamp
gracelessly
beckons.

To confuse this kind of inanity with poetry is to do an enormous disservice to any student who may be trying to understand the nature of poetry. As far as the nature of the computer is concerned, the "poems" might be brought front and center to hammer home the axiom "garbage in, garbage out," but the spirit of the article is quite otherwise. What is worst of all, the appearance of such an article, in a journal prepared under highly regarded auspices for the better illumination of secondary-school teaching, betrays an educational system in utter disarray.

The consequences are far-reaching. The bread-and-butter of expository writing is the simple declarative sentence. It was once a truism within journalism that from three to six months of unrelieved effort are required to teach the ordinary college graduate to write a simple declarative sentence. A city editor of my acquaintance once remarked: "There are at least a thousand right ways to write a news story, and one wrong way. A cub reporter can always be depended on to find that one wrong way." That much the English teachers have achieved.

None the less, people do learn to write acceptable expository prose, and better. They do so because a good many people become quickly aware that there is a great deal of satisfaction to be derived from the production of workmanlike writing. To a surprisingly large degree, the answer to the question posed in this chapter is as simple as that: they write because they like to write, or perhaps more accurately in most instances like to have written, since the pleasure lies in the product rather than the performance. (It may very well be the other way around for the creative writer, who if he is any good at all is likely to be disappointed in the product.)

The spirit is that of any craftsman. Once more I return to Genesis, where God the Lexicographer is also God the Craftsman: "And God called the dry land Earth; and the gathering together of the waters called he Seas: and God saw that it was good." No more anthropomorphic a creator could be conceived.

Clearly, what is concerned is far more than a willingness to write. Such a willingness can be engendered by a clear perception that writing is a direct path to some goal or another that lies quite outside the writing itself: a means to an end. There is an obvious distinction to be made between a scholar, or a feminist, or a political radical, who is a writer, and a writer who is a scholar, or a feminist, or a political radical. The difference lies in the manner in which he directs his efforts when the two roles conflict, as they very occasionally do: which role he subordinates if subordinate he must.

In the preceding chapter, the writer was described as his own prime audience, to whom at the outset all his efforts are directed. If his temperament so dictates, he may also be his own ultimate audience, to whom at the end all his efforts have been directed; all his other audiences are eavesdroppers, and if they are willing to pay for the privilege, so much the better.

It is not all clear water. Writing for self-satisfaction, the writer can quickly become self-indulgent if he is not on guard, and self-indulgent writing, whatever else it may be (and it may be Marcel Proust or James Joyce), is not expository writing. Reasonably or not, I find myself incapable of conceiving expository writing, or any serious writing at all, which is directed solely and finally at the writer himself, and I believe that an expository writer must feel some responsibility toward that broader audience even though it may be no more than an audience of one. Once again, I am defining the craftsman. Those are credos, but so is a good deal more that I have written here, and I make no apology.

"To whom," it seems, leads to a conclusion that could not be immediately anticipated, and like any good question leads also to other questions. The expository writer, it begins to appear, is best served if the fates or the genetic laws have endowed him at once with the temperament of a craftsman and the capacity to derive satisfaction from the synthesis of words into written language. I do not want to imply that these two characteristics are either necessary or sufficient. Craftsmanship alone will go a long way even for one who writes unwillingly, and so will sheer eagerness to put words on paper and read them critically, for a certain amount of craftsmanship (unlike any amount of artistry) can be taught. But if those temperamental characteristics are present at the outset, the expository writer is off to the best possible start.

My own biases are being exposed shamelessly, and I am well aware of it. I have arbitrarily defined *expository writing* in a fashion that excludes a great deal commonly considered to fall within the domain of the phrase: such writing as fills large elegant tomes dealing with health diets, the yearnings and strivings of film stars, and optimum behavior in the privacy of the bedroom. To cast that statement in another and perhaps clearer form, I have pitched out of the canon most of the expository writing that directly generates large financial returns. The sort of writer I have implicitly described is not very likely to win a place among the much esteemed filthy rich out of the sales of books and magazine articles and television series that ruthlessly expose the cosmos.

Considering the body of practitioners as a whole, that is not a matter of great significance. Most of them are occupied with the requirements of the very small and differentiated audience, and have neither the time nor the inclination to put all that aside for hazardous ventures into the world of commercial publishing. Yet there are a few, clearly masters of the tools that one must employ to meet the needs of the larger audiences, who none the less persist in turning out articles and books that could not possibly appeal to more than a paltry few thousand readers.

The answer lies, I suspect, in the extremely close connection of expository writing with the process of taking thought. For reasons which appear to lie somewhere beyond human comprehension, it seems undignified to *think* for money, although short of such activities as running heroin and the like, it seems quite respectable to earn it in any other fashion, and certainly by writing. The general attitude appears to be that taking thought, when it is well conducted, will be rewarded by respect rather than cold cash. That, after all, is a homage to thinking as a quintessentially human undertaking that transcends the common marketplace. I would look upon it as a considerable homage, and a considerable payment.

Writers are no less materialistic than any of the rest of us, but much of that attitude appears to rub off on the expository writer. His craft is writing, and he is not likely to be as powerful a thinker as a man whose craft, or art, is thinking. Still, by virtue of what he does he is at worst an associate member of the association of thinkers, entitled to show up at meetings as long as he remains quiet, and to participate in the annual outing.

Why, then, does he work at writing? For just those reasons that lead a man to work at thinking: because it is what he likes to do, generally, but beyond that for respect. In part the respect of the audience he addresses, small as it may be, and possibly in even larger part his own self-respect. "What profiteth it a man if he gaineth great wealth," asks the Good Book, "and loseth thereby his soul?" The answer is that it profiteth him a good deal, but for some folks not quite enough.

I am not trying to ennoble my own caste. Writers may, and do, write because some odd configuration of their genes makes it possible for them to earn a living in that fashion and not in any other; others because they drifted into writing and somehow managed to learn how. And I did not say, after all, that expository writers are noble by nature; only that a certain attitude seemed to rub off on them.

Let me, with considerable hesitation, inject what may appear an odd personal note; it seems to me to illustrate much of what I have been writing. I began my own career as a journalist. In general, journalists have tended to be a somewhat loutish, liquorish and lecherous lot, and in my day no better educated than paid. Yet I was aware from the outset of a deep sense of responsibility pervading the city room. It rarely extended beyond the city room. One of the newspapers for which I worked was as corrupt as a newspaper could be, and the editorial staff was engaged in an endless struggle to vitiate that corruption. Odd working conditions.

I wondered then, and have wondered now for a good many years, what had brought into being in a most unlikely body of men that deep sense of responsibility. (In the later of those years, I have wondered where it has gone.) It was through the very act of outlining and then writing this chapter that I have begun to understand. We were writers, and a certain part of what goes into writing rubbed off on us. Unrespectable as we may have been, we wanted the respect of our audience and our own respect, and we went so far as to plot against our publishers, when that was necessary, to get it.

Television converted the journalist who made his way to what is conceived to be the top of his craft from writer to performer, whether as anchorman on television or "investigative reporter" in print. He moved ahead on the basis not of what he wrote but of how he appeared. And what rubbed off on him now was not a desire for respect but some other kinds of desire: perhaps the desire to be adulated, or envied, or to mix with those who are adulated and envied, or in a few instances perhaps simply to be rich.

The hypothesis is shaky at best, and perhaps not persuasive, for it smacks of nostalgia and the general sense of grievance that arises with the passage of years. I include it here as a contribution not to the theory of journalism but to the practice of expository writing, at the heart of which there lies, for better or worse, the process of taking thought.

Samuel Johnson's great dictionary defined one kind of expository writer as "an underpaid wretch" (and you have seen at the head of this chapter a related dyspepsia). In his own days he was no doubt accurate about the underpayment. In these days, with the hunger for skills in the use of the written word, it is accurate no longer. The writer is far from the most highly rewarded member of society, but without excessive good fortune he can count on three square meals a day and a warm bed at night, along with associated fringe benefits.

He also is rewarded, and occasionally amused, by the exercise of a power he may not have earned but that goes with the job. An early mentor advised me once that "the man who holds the chalk runs the meeting." It was long ago, in the days of blackboards, but the aphorism is readily brought up to date. Frequently the man who prepares the document governs the course that an ensuing discussion will take, and to that extent affects the decision that is ultimately taken.

But these are by-products, and not the central matters. About those central matters nothing can be said beyond the general assertion that the individual writer will have his own reasons for writing, and that once he has begun writing, other reasons will occur to him. The grain of good sense that lies in Sam Johnson's remarks is that he is not likely to write for no reason at all.

Chapter Thirteen

And Finally, How?

Taffeta phrases, silken terms precise,
Three-piled hyperboles, spruce affectation,
Figures pedantical . . .

WILLIAM SHAKESPEARE, Love's Labour's Lost

F<small>ROM</small> beginning to end, the writer is called upon to make decisions. At the lowest levels—which does not necessarily signify the easiest levels—he chooses from among the letters, the phrases, the punctuation, and the sentence structures and other syntactical devices he has at his command. At the higher levels, he must decide what he wishes to say, to which audience he is addressing himself, and just why he is doing all this in the first place.

The sum of all these decisions constitutes the writer's style, and creates the tone that is set by the finished product. *Style* and *tone*, as I use the words, are more or less opposite sides of the same coin: *style* is what the writer imposes on his writing; *tone* is what the reader finds there. The writer's final task is to assure a correspondence between the style he adopts and the tone he intends. There are no guarantees.

Leaving aside the prodigies who can speak in all tongues, most writers have at their command a limited range of styles which reduces, at the limit, to but a single style in certain extremely capable and even extremely talented people. Indeed, a very successful writer is likely to adopt a single style and abide by it, partly on the principle that what works should not be fixed, but also because a very successful writer has created expectations in his readers that he is reluctant to disappoint. It is not disabling: when Art Buchwald wants to be deadly serious he can manage it superbly without departing very far from his customary style.

Up to a certain point, a practiced writer can develop a family of styles. The decisions that he makes with respect to the audience he is addressing—just who it is, just what he wishes to say to it or (more broadly) how he wishes to affect it, just why he is going to all that trouble—will lead to a final decision: just how he is to respond most effectively to conditions he himself has brought into being. The style he adopts, or seeks to adopt, reflects that final decision.

The response, however, is not entirely free. The ordinary humans among us cannot change their vocabularies or their syntax with complete abandon between assignments. Our body of knowledge can be extended, but not entirely renewed; our biases may change with time, but at any moment they are stubborn and resistant. In short, even the wide range of styles that a writer may possess is likely to fall into a family of styles that characterizes that writer, and that in the end is the consequence of his own personality.

Here lie dragons. The personality that creates the style belongs to the man doing the writing. Since he writes what he likes, he is prepared to like what he writes. But writing is above all an activity over which a critical mind must preside, and affection tends to dull the critical mind. Under such circumstances, style threatens to become habit; habit becomes indulgence; indulgence leads to excess. In the end, one finds the writer who is no longer portraying himself, but parodying himself.

No one writing regularly, and certainly no one writing on demand, can afford to ignore the danger. Earlier I alluded to formula writing, in words that surely signified that such writing occupied no high place in my esteem. I was thinking, of course, of the uncreative creative writer, who writes that one time-tested romance again and again. But the expository writer can also be a formula writer, in terms of style rather than content (although the two can also go together), and the consequences are quite as lamentable.

For the moment, the pathologies can be ignored. (But only for the moment.) The assumption must be that writing need not suffer from them, although it frequently will, and we can go forward with consideration of the process by means of which style in any given instance is determined, or essayed.

I will be forgiven if I select for scrutiny an example with which I am reasonably familiar, and which has the further advantage of lying close at hand, by which I mean my very own writing.

The sequence that appears here in the most recent chapters proceeds from *what* to *whom,* and from *whom* to *why.* It is the logical sequence, but not necessarily or even very often the temporal sequence. The temporal sequence, moreover, is not nearly as tidy.

This book began with *why.* I have been convinced for many years that a most important skill, that of ordinary expository writing, is no longer held in respect and that in consequence there has been a general deterioration in the practice of that skill. The deterioration, moreover, is taking place in a period when growing numbers of men and women are being called upon to communicate information by means of the written word. To call such a state of affairs unhealthy does not appear excessive.

Those judgments are widely shared. Commissions are created at regular intervals to examine them and reinforce them; the periodical press asserts them with accompanying lament, the public at large has been known to gossip about the matter at cocktail parties and other ritual occasions. At the same time, there is no persuasive evidence that any of those honorable institutions and individuals have any clear knowledge of just what it is that they are lamenting the lack of. The nature of the written word, and of the process which created it, is almost completely absent from the discussion, because it is not understood. When it does enter, the terms are irrelevant, or suggest that the craft of expository writing lies principally in avoiding sentences which conclude: "lamenting the lack of." (I do not deny, however, that such sentences should be avoided.)

There is also the manner in which "writing" is taught in the schools. It is now subsumed under "communications arts," which includes eight-millimeter film and the like, and offered to students in a form which conceals or distorts the process beyond any point at which it would be recognizable to those who actually perform it. This I learned in some detail in the course of activities associated with my employment as officer of a philanthropic foundation.

Finally, it is a matter that, rightly or wrongly, I think I know something about. As I noted in setting forth my credentials, I have done during my lifetime an enormous amount of expository writing, in almost all known modes and perhaps one or two I invented. Since I am by nature rather introspective, I have tended to think about what I was doing. Also, I have on the whole been modestly well paid along the way, which suggests that my writing was weighed in the balance from time to time and found at least good enough for all practical purposes.

Putting it all together, and without any tendency toward messianism of which I was aware, I decided that writing a book on the general subject of the written word would be a responsible thing to do, and relieve me of any obligation to fulfill my civic duties by marching in antinuclear demonstrations, helping save the whale, or abusing people who smoke in restaurants.

There was also a modest side. Thoughts about the written word, of some of which I was quite proud, milled around in my head, but whether they were coherent thoughts, and how well they would bear examination, I simply was not certain. Writing at length about writing was the best way I knew to straighten the matter

out, and I was anxious to do it. I would be writing, in short, for
self-satisfaction.

All that provided the *why,* and what followed immediately
were details: I found I had the time; bought ten floppy diskettes,
which I proposed to use to store each word and phrase as it poured
into my word processor and out again; and sharpened several
dozen pencils, which I did not propose to use at all.

The determination of *why* went a long way toward determining
whom, as is generally the case. There was, I knew, an enormously
large audience out there who considered themselves expert in the
matter of the written word; indeed, an audience very nearly coex-
tensive with the total adult population, counting this country
alone, and no doubt spilling over into other countries sharing the
British heritage one way or another. Most of that audience, however, was made up of people to whom the euphemism "functionally illiterate" might well be applied, since they were not accustomed to reading books intended seriously and for the most part
not accustomed to reading books at all. As for books some of them
might read, I was not accustomed to writing such books, and in any
case such a book would not serve the second of my purposes,
which was self-satisfaction.

The loss of that splendidly numerous audience, to which I had
been resigned at the outset, left me only differentiated audiences
to consider. That led immediately to the horrible realization that
the book would not make me independently wealthy. It took quite
a while and a considerable consumption of alcohol before I was
resigned to that fact, but I happened to be in a saloon at the time,
and the pain was minimal.

There was a quite dissimilar second expert audience to be considered, the experts in this instance possessing the appropriate
credentials in the form of variously defined doctoral degrees. I was
persuaded that some might begin to read a book called *The Written Word,* but few would pass beyond the first few pages, and most
of those only because they enjoyed being whipped into a state of

fury. There are exceptions, of course, but most scholars consider it infra dig to read unscholarly books in their own and allied disciplines and would very much like to make it illegal to write them, although thanks to the First Amendment they cannot as yet lay a glove on me. Their interests, too, tend to be narrow: the expert on transformational grammar is not terribly concerned with the manner in which garden-variety grammar is actually employed.

Something called "composition" or the like may very well be the most taught academic subject in the United States. It begins in the elementary schools somewhere in the neighborhood of the second grade, continues through all the years of secondary school and college, and is to be found even in graduate schools, where it goes by the name of "remedial writing" or an apologetic alternative of one kind or another. Thereafter it is a mainstay of Adult or Continuing or Extension Education. Outside the schools, it is taught by correspondence, and although I have never seen a writing course on television I am certain there must be one. (In that last instance, it is almost always creative writing that is being taught, but occasionally the course is intended to serve more mundane aspirations.)

Lots of courses signifies lots of students and lots of teachers, and consequently lots of textbooks; perhaps I had been hasty back there in the saloon. But I run afoul of the experts again, for I do not have the credentials to write a textbook, and without credentials the book could not possibly be adopted. Neither do I have the teaching experience, without which the book would be at best fraudulent.

I am left, then, with a small but select audience. I write for those who share with me a belief that writing is important and are willing to think about the matter seriously and more fully. Some will be teachers of "composition" and some simply teachers; most will be neither. Few will be writers. All will be readers, and most will have read widely and seriously. Any difficulties I have in communicating with that audience will be of my own making.

The monetary rewards will be small. In terms of the labor to which I have committed myself, negligible; in the same time and with a good deal less effort there is considerably more to be earned as a filing clerk. Certainly, writing the book I have in mind is not the sort of thing I would undertake if I thought of it as drudgery. I must enjoy it.

In all, I find the audience quite satisfactory. I have addressed larger audiences, but not very frequently since I abandoned journalism, and I left journalism primarily because I preferred the differentiated audience. Mostly since then I have addressed far smaller audiences, but aside from size they were generally much like this one. All in all, I am on familiar ground and doing what I enjoy doing.

I recount all this at such great length because the choice or the evaluation of audience is the most important of the choices that a writer self-consciously makes. Both the *why* and the *what* take care of themselves in their own fashions. The *why* usually grows cumulatively and over time, almost without conscious purpose, for an exercise of this kind. Alternatively it may be stimulated by an assignment of some kind or by a conversation with a publisher, but unless the goal is entirely or predominantly measured in dollars and cents, the assignment will not be undertaken or the conversation pursued unless it resonates with something or other that is already in the writer's mind. In those circumstances he may not single-handedly select his audience, but he must go through much the same steps to take the measure of the audience toward which his efforts are going to be directed.

Until that stage is passed, the *what* is only dimly perceived. The writer himself may not be entirely aware of the fragility of his earlier thoughts on the matter, but he finds it out the moment he begins shaping his document in his mind, and the true size of the task becomes evident as soon as he sets out to create an outline, first in his mind and then on a sheet of paper. But I am repeating myself. Writing of this sort is itself the very act of taking thought. That is the central theme of much I have been trying to convey.

Those three decisions—for they are all decisions, although they stand at different levels—together with the writer's own personality, combine to determine the style in which the document is couched. The manner in which he expresses himself represents his own response to the demands made upon him by his subject, his audience and his intentions. Other decisions would create a quite different set of demands, a quite different response and (since his own personality remains unchanged) no more than a somewhat different style.

In the light of the decisions that are represented in this document, the first obligation to which I would pay allegiance was immediately obvious. The book would be courteous. I use the adjective in a somewhat uncommon sense, to which I was first introduced by Jerome Bruner (credit where credit is due), who invented it for his own purposes. Education, he said, should be courteous, in the sense that it attributed to those being educated a degree of knowledge, sensitivity and dignity that in actual fact they might not possess. That usage is in fact somewhat too sharp for my own needs, since I can presume that the audience I have specified does have sensitivity and dignity. It has knowledge as well, but not precisely the body of knowledge I have, for no two persons have precisely the same body of knowledge. More knowledge, quite possibly, but not the same.

We strike a bargain, my audience and I. They will concede, if only for the moment, that I may have some special knowledge of writing. I will assume that in other matters they have more knowledge than I. Consequently I will not patronize my audience in terms of vocabulary, and I will assume that they will comprehend any allusions I make, unless that vocabulary and those allusions are hopelessly arcane. I earlier twice used the sentence "My withers are unwrung." Most of my audience will recognize it, and enjoy a feeling of kinship. Most of the rest will be curious, and perhaps make some small effort to puzzle out my choice of that particular sentence. Few will be annoyed, and they are likely to comprehend the next allusion, which makes up for it.

The substance of the document is largely opinion—<u>my</u> opinion, although I hope others share the opinions and still others will by reason of my efforts see the light. In any case, that characteristic led me to decide that I would write the book in the first person, and that when I drew upon relevant personal experience I would not be hesitant about revealing it.

Considering the *why* of the document, as I have determined it, I am pressing a cause and I seek allies. As a consequence, I have been quite as generous with the words *you* and *we* as with the word *I*. It is no more than a literary device, to be sure, but I choose to address my audience directly, so that they become fellows and not merely readers.

All this goes to make a conversational style, which brings along with it still other characteristics. No one in the large wide world writes as he speaks, or could do so however hard he tried. It is possible, however, to simulate the effect, by the judicious use of words and grammatical structures that are more commonly found in speech than in the written word. "Defective" sentences, for example. An occasional sally into slang. The choice of idiomatic rather than formal statement.

The conversational style is simulated in still another sense. A speaker engaged in a real conversation acts within a rigid framework of time. Anything he may say must either precede or succeed anything else he may say. It may not be recalled that way, but it happens that way.

The conversational style, however, is fraudulent. A good many pages back, for example, I used the word *lapidary* and indicated, as I very well might in relaxed conversation, that I was really not quite sure what it meant, although in fact my years of obligatory dedication to the study of Latin provided a clue. I said at the time I would look it up, and did. The OED told me that it means, among other things, "fit to be carved on stone."

A quite satisfactory outcome, since that is what I thought it meant when I wrote it. But if the OED had a different story to tell, the word *lapidary* would not appear in that sentence, and this explanation would not appear here. The writer, in short, need never say, "I wish I could take that back," for he can. Indeed, he must, over and over again.

The conversational style is as much an artifact as any other literary style; as much an artifact as what the writer ultimately delivers. Pretending to be in a temporal framework, it provides a semblance of spontaneity which is entirely counterfeit. In all likelihood, the sentences and paragraphs that appear to the reader most spontaneous are those over which the writer has labored most diligently. Fraud or not, that is his vocation, and it is no sin for a man to labor at his vocation.

What I have given here is merely the broad structure of the style adopted for this very book. The manner in which the details are worked out is also a matter of style. I do not work it out as another writer would, nor could I. "Style is the man himself," said Buffon.

It is obvious that the structure of the style adopted here would be a disastrous mistake if I were attempting to produce a learned book for a learned audience. Such a book is written for quite different reasons and directed to a quite different constituency, which has criteria of its own upon which it judges learned books. In principle, such an audience is interested in hard fact or in hypothesis closely reasoned from hard fact, and will not tolerate a mere statement of opinion. As a consequence, all kinds of devices are adopted to avoid the impression that an opinion is being put forward, although it very often is and the devices themselves are often laughable.

Under those circumstances, the word *I* is eschewed at any cost, replaced by "It is noted that . . . " or "The following experiment was performed . . . " or "Present opinion holds . . . " The language is at best formal, and more often pure jargon so that the author may be clearly identified as a member of the guild. Allusions are shunned in favor of citations, or if an allusion creeps in it will be something dependably familiar to any given expert at any given moment. It is the sort of writing that begs to be done badly, although like any other writing it can be done well. It is also the sort of writing that infects people who are not learned at all but believe something is to be gained by appearing learned. Bad journalism is full of it.

Yet even that sort of writing is likely to portray the man who wrote it, particularly if he is a prolific writer. Formalized as it is, there will be within it the systematic choice of words, or phrasing, or attitude, that bespeaks the author. It will be more persistent in one who writes willingly, but even under compulsion the style of the writer will come through.

I have acknowledged my inability to write a learned book on the written word, but that does not necessarily signify an inability to write any learned book at all. I can, and have, although it is my misfortune, I suppose, that I am truly learned only upon a single and a trivial subject. I have written such a book on contract bridge and I am half author of another; I have also contributed to still others.

All that writing is in the learned style. It meets all the criteria: careful in its citations, scrupulous in at least the pretense of objectivity, carrying all the stigmata of authenticity. All the same, I am certain—indeed, I am often reminded—that those who know any large part of the body of my writing will recognize me in the book I wrote in its entirety, and in the appropriate portions of the others.

I concede that there are some who are chameleons. Speechwriters pretty much must be, unless the person for whom the speeches are being written is willing to subordinate his own personality to that of the writer. But most of us can do no more than camouflage our styles. The perceptive eye will still see the reality. In a way, it is good for the ego. What we write, in the end, is ours.

I have been dealing here with the structure of a writer's style, and at least nodded in the direction of the brickwork, by which I mean such matters as vocabulary and syntax. Something more must be touched on lightly, along with an excuse for doing no more than touch at this moment.

Holding stubbornly to my metaphor, I must remind you that building often has ornamentation and superfluities: the statuary of old cathedrals and the gargoyles that came with it, or in more modern terms the atria in latter-day office buildings and the structural members which support nothing at all. Despite the dismissive manner of the description, those elements do add grace to the building in accordance with the fashion of the times, and I suppose that the vacuous structural members add confidence. There is, of course, the danger that when the fashion passes they will look odd and out of place.

That very paragraph is an example of what I have in mind where writing is concerned. The first sentence might well end with "superfluities," for what it has to say will remain intact. The second sentence might begin with "Those elements," since the preceding words deal not with the matter at hand but with the manner of its presentation. Still, they are intended to add a certain amount of grace and to instill confidence, and if they do so they serve useful purposes.

Those ornaments and superfluities, and at least one other of them, which is also represented in the last few sentences and which you may already have discovered, happen to be part of my own writing style. I am fully aware of them, and they frighten me, for I am aware also that it is easy to fall into a pattern of excessive use, annoying to the reader and suggestive of auto-parody, as I have said.

Judiciousness is called for. I do not happen to like the bare style, although I know its virtues and I am also not beyond using it for contrast. I know, in an abstract sort of way, a good many other stylistic habits from which my colleagues benefit or suffer, as the case may be, and I am not above using them as well, when it appears to me to be the reasonable thing to do, although they are not my style. What makes them different, as far as I am concerned, is that I am not likely to overuse them. They are a resource which I may or may not use sagaciously, but they do not menace me. My own stylistic habits do, and I know it.

The writer's first obligation is a sensitivity to his own stylistic habits, and a healthy distrust of those habits. He should not abandon them, and indeed I am by no means certain that a writer can, but neither should he become enamored of them, or become their victim. He should know them, and know them even better than those who are likely to criticize them, and he should be wary.

Above all, those stylistic habits must be in the forefront of the writer's mind when he settles down to the arduous process of revision. Because the process of revision is so much a process of guarding against stylistic excesses, I propose to deal further with style in the context of revision, which will occupy us in the pages ahead.

I have an uneasy feeling that these last pages produce intimations of inconsistency. I may appear to be saying that a writer is at once a slave to the style with which he is somehow or other endowed, and at the same time a calculating craftsman creating his style as he goes along. If it is an inconsistency, it is no more than what we human beings must expect. There is a tension in all of us between what we are and what we would want to be. In the writer, it takes the form of a tension between how he writes and how he would want to write. I suppose that somewhere there are writers who can look upon their products and say, "It is exactly as I wanted it to be." I have never met one.

Chapter Fourteen

Revision

> In composing, as a general rule, run your pen
> through every other word you have written;
> you have no idea what vigor it will give your
> style.
>
> SYDNEY SMITH, Recipe for Salad

No TWO WRITERS are likely to go about their business in exactly the same way. There are those, of whom I am one, who follow the sage advice of Lewis Carroll: they begin at the beginning, and go on until they come to the end. Carroll's counsel, of course, did not conclude there; he felt obliged to add "and then stop," but that is a luxury denied the writer, for only when a writer's task has come to the end does he set to work in earnest.

Others slice their work into blocks, writing a few thousand words, revising them carefully, and going on to the next few thousand. I have taken no polls, largely because writers do not ordinarily speak to each other, but I do not believe that to be a common procedure except in documents such as some scholarly works and most textbooks, which fall naturally into discrete sections demanding that one be completed before the next can be undertaken. Even then, the point comes when the manuscript must be regarded as a whole, if it carries any kind of continuous line of thought. For all of us, sooner or later the manuscript must be read as a unit, from start to finish. The reading generally begins in a flush of great elation, which immediately passes.

None the less, what the writer has achieved is of great significance. We have agreed he is not a *creative* writer, but that is conventional, like all meanings. Beyond any doubt, he has created an object. The manuscript before him began in the corners of his mind, as a somewhat chaotic configuration of thoughts and fancies and shapeless notions, or words and phrases and sentences, of forebodings and aspirations, and surely of purpose. All of that he has converted into a *thing.* It can be observed, studied from whatever perspective he may choose, altered and restored, passed from hand to hand. It has an existence independent of his own; it has passed from parasitism to symbiosis. Any hand can improve it, or build upon it.

Clearly no small achievement. The universe of objects has an inhabitant it was formerly without. It has a potential it formerly lacked. It is a marvelous culmination.

That is one way to look at the matter, and quite reasonable. But from another point of view, the object that the writer has brought into being is a good deal less a culmination than a point of departure. The manuscript over which he has labored so devotedly over so long a period the writer now fears will turn out to be a dreary waste of undigested fancies expressed in slovenly prose. As a whole, he begins to suspect, it lacks rhyme or reason; in detail it is blurred where it is not positively obscure; the fine strokes are revealed to be infantile and the picture viewed as a whole is the product of senility. All is to do over again.

That immediate impression, of course, is as false as the sense of completion that preceded it. A competent writer will ordinarily turn out a competent manuscript. But competent is not ever enough, and the blemishes have to be removed, as far as it lies within the writer's power.

At this very moment, too, the craftsman is distinguished from the dilettante in a somewhat unexpected way. The dilettante is inclined to cradle his manuscript in his arms, protecting it from enemies without. The craftsman seizes the opportunity to send it out into the world and see how it fares. He does not have to be told that the manuscript cries out for revision; he knows that, and indeed he expected it. He is fully prepared to revise. What he wants is assistance.

In some respects, the writer is in the worst possible position to undertake the task he faces. For months on end he has been struggling to achieve lucidity, for lucidity is the one single characteristic over which no bargaining is possible. The very fierceness of the struggle is such as to encourage him to believe he has won his way to lucidity. Certainly, once that initial surge of doubt has subsided, each sentence and phrase he has written appears to possess the brittle sharpness and the cold clarity of spring water. It should. He has been living with those sentences and phrases for months on end. It is not at all surprising that he should know, down to the last tendril of subtlety, exactly what they mean. Whether he has communicated that knowledge is another matter altogether.

The writer must grit his teeth and set himself to ferreting out obscurity wherever it may be found. In particular, he must listen to the sound of his sentences. Misreadings do not come from words and sentences in themselves, but from miscomprehensions of the status of the word within the sentence. The significance of almost any sentence of more than a few words can be altered out of all recognition by the tone and tempo and cadences that a speaker may impose on it. The sentence, furthermore, cannot be read without some tone and tempo and cadence, however bland or minimal. The fundamental task of the writer is to impose upon the sentence, by the devices of the written language and with no other resource, the sound that will carry the meaning he intends. He cannot do that as long as he believes that the sound *he* hears when he reads the sentence is the sound all men must hear. He must learn to recognize the latent treachery of words he himself set down.

What is so difficult for the writer, however, is simplicity itself for those inclined to be supportive, and still simpler for those inclined otherwise. They come to the sentences fresh, his friends with no important preconceptions and the rest looking for trouble and thereby converting themselves into friends for his immediate purposes. They will find ambiguities that the writer could not possibly have identified. What is more, the presumption must be that they will never be wrong. (It is a false presumption, but a healthy one, and in any case inescapable.)

Those readers will provide other services as well. They will laboriously correct typographical errors, misspellings, and minor grammatical lapses some of which are not lapses at all. All those incidental mishaps would of course have been discovered and corrected at some stage or another in the normal course of events, and a few new ones will slip in to take their place, but the polite writer thanks the reader anyway. Not effusively. A simple "thanks" will do.

All this might be called the search for mechanical lucidity, for it is concerned almost entirely with the bare mechanics of writing. It is a search that can never be completed, but with time and patience it can be carried to a point where those demands of the language have been satisfied. A good deal will thereby be accomplished, but a good deal will also remain.

To a man, these early readers are almost certain to assure the writer that he has written an "absolutely brilliant" whatever. All such encomia are the small change of social intercourse. They buy nothing, but they jingle nicely in the pocket. Treasure them, but do not try to spend them.

The good reader, of course, will provide a good deal of help. He will read the manuscript attentively, think hard about it, and set himself to judging it and criticizing it. A writer should have the good sense to appreciate the help he is getting, the ability to improve his manuscript as a consequence of the criticism, and the confidence to ignore criticism that seems to him to be misguided.

We agreed a long way back, or at any rate I agreed, that what we are dealing with as expository writers are description and criticism, or description and argument. I am sure that a dictionary authorizes the view that lucidity does not imply either verisimilitude in description or cogency in argument; that an assertion of either sort can at the same time be utterly lucid and utterly wrong. I am none the less persuaded that there is implied a higher level of lucidity at which the purposes of lucidity as well as the mechanics are taken into consideration. That kind of lucidity, too, is the business of the expository writer.

It was stipulated at the outset that we would be dealing with writing that was both serious and at least moderately extensive. Fragments have their place, but there is not much that can be usefully said about them in isolation. Yet if fragments are collected into a book (signed Eric Hoffer, perhaps, or Nietzsche) they are perceived in a different light; there is an implication of order and coherence in the very act of collection. (None of this is to be construed as an endorsement of either Hoffer or Nietzsche.)

The outlining procedure upon which I was so insistent is of course a process of creating order and coherence. Whether or not a formal outline is produced is a tactical matter and nothing more. The search for order and coherence continues in any event; it is what we call *thinking*. When it employs the written word beyond the manufacture of an outline, it is called *writing*.

Whatever it may be called, it becomes more difficult as its scope widens. Widened scope means greater complexity upon which to impose order, and more nodes to provide the coherence being sought. The task is for most of us infinitely more manageable when writing is called in to assist, but the writing does not spring into being all of a piece. It must be achieved, with labor and over time.

As a practical matter, what needs to be done is done piecemeal. Small islands of order and coherence are created, and perhaps an archipelago here and there. It is not surprising that when the document as a whole is examined, the impression is not one of order and coherence at all, any more than many islands make a mainland. And only on a mainland is it possible to go smoothly and confidently from one point to the next.

Because the writer is concerned with order and coherence at

every stage, it comes as a surprise to find that in the large it does not exist at all in his manuscript. There are portions of the argument missing (if for the moment I may call it an argument, as more often than not it is) and other portions present but misplaced. Worst of all, there are arguments that are quite coherent in their place, but that simply will not fit together.

The explicit purpose of the outline was to prevent all these disasters, and a good outline prevents a good many of them. But the disasters often appear only when the detail is provided, and an outline that tried to deal with detail would be a manuscript, and no longer an outline at all.

The journalist, always pressed for time, quickly learns to deal with the problem. He becomes proficient at what is called "writing around" the open water. When it is done skillfully, the inattentive reader will always be deceived, and even the attentive reader may have trouble locating the lacunae. Bridges are seen where they were never seen before, and it is not immediately apparent that they carry no load. It is precisely that sort of thing that leads to the connotations of *journalistic.*

If more than journalism is intended, the manuscript must in some degree be rebuilt. The missing arguments must be provided, and the presentation reordered for maximum clarity. There will be times when that stage of writing will reveal that an important link in the chain of reasoning does not appear and indeed may not exist, which means either that the whole chain of reasoning is unsound or that the writer has not yet completed the task of thinking it through. What happens next is between the writer and his maker: he can write around the missing link, or apologize for it and express the belief it will one day be found, or abandon the enterprise altogether. I do not know that the last of these has ever been the recourse of choice, but I suppose it has happened. In any case, the problem is no different from those a lawyer faces as part of his daily routine.

As for order, the universe itself is untidy, and we are all prepared to live with a certain amount of untidiness just as we live

with a certain amount of unfairness. All we ask of a writer is that
he maximize the orderliness of his document, which means working at it until he is convinced he is making no further progress.

All this has been in terms of argument, but something parallel
can arise when the manuscript deals primarily with what we have
been calling description. Some hard facts important to the document as a whole are found absent without leave as the revision
proceeds, and it is a glaring absence. During revision, that kind of
discovery is far more frequently encountered than the fatal flaw
in the argument.

As often as not the situation arises because the writer, in the heat
of composition, does not wish to be bothered with facts. As the
vernacular has it, he is on a roll. He proceeds in the faith that when
the time comes to revise he will find the facts, or that in a pinch
he will make do without some fact or another that he would love
to possess. For the moment he simply assumes it, and presses
ahead.

Depending upon the importance of the missing fact, the profundity of the writer's scruples and his estimate of the likelihood of
detection, the assumption may still be there, unidentified as such,
when the manuscript is sent along to the publisher. Under certain
circumstances, as when a man is writing a research report for
the Journal of the American Medical Association, it is enough to
have him drummed out of the guild, if discovered.

But as a general matter it is not nearly as serious as it sounds.
No one knows everything and certainly there is not always time
to find all one would wish to know. A serious effort during the
period of revision is always called for if the writer is an honest man.
Failing, he may decide to continue on the basis of the assumption, in the faith that the fact is there to be found somewhere or
other.

Earlier in this book you will find an allusion to a portion of a
sermon delivered some three hundred–odd years ago by John
Donne. I wrote it aware that although I was certain that the
sermon in question was the work of one British dominie or an-

other, I was by no means sure that John Donne was the man. While I was revising the manuscript, I spent a good many hours searching through the sermons of John Donne—an activity I recommend to no one—and took other steps as well, all without success. The allusion is still there. Sue me. I can predict with some assurance that I will be put in possession of the fact I seek, no doubt somewhat abusively, shortly after the book is published, and thereby made an honest man retroactively.

The least of the problems encountered during revision, as I have already intimated, are those which seem most to fascinate the pedagogue. There are matters of grammar and syntax about which I am uncertain, and as a general rule when such uncertainty arises during revision I attempt to puzzle out the problem, as I usually can, or to find out what the canonical form may be, which can be somewhat more difficult.

The number of people passionately devoted to grammar and syntax, however, is beyond belief. Friends and others to whom I will have circulated the manuscript will clutter the margins with corrections where they find it appropriate to do so, and I am aware also that somewhere down the line there are editors and professional proofreaders lying in wait. Grammar and syntax will certainly be paid the deference to which they are entitled, and spelling as well.

The real problem lies elsewhere. My written grammar and syntax are a good deal more conservative than my spoken syntax and grammar. The word *whom* is one I use in the spoken language only when it follows immediately upon a preposition: I say "to whom" and "for whom," but I would not dream of saying "Whom did you give it to" or " . . . buy it for." That usage in spoken English is wrong, and that is all there is to it. In the written language it is still correct, and I honor it.

But conservatism is relative. As far as I am concerned, for example, the subjunctive has vanished, except for certain relics here and there, as in "If I were king." Even in the written language it is an affectation. I ignore the "correction" when it is made in the margin, and fight it when it is made by editors and proofreaders.

There are writers for whom I have great respect, and who would disagree. That is quite as it should be. The language is a living thing, and at the margins of change the decision to go one way or another is a personal decision. I have confidence in my own usages, and they have confidence in theirs, and that is as it should be. Deep down, I also believe I am using the language—the living language—as it should be used, but so do they. I do not for one moment believe that there is an authority to whom we can go for judgment, for to do so is a denial that the language is alive, and I cannot drum up any deep interest in a dead language to be employed for purposes of thought or of communication. I will write the language I know, and I do not propose to apologize for it.

The final task of revision is the most difficult of all, and also a task in which neither friends nor enemies are likely to be nearly as helpful as they might be. Having satisfied himself that the manuscript is lucid, coherent and orderly, the writer is obliged to examine its style and tone. This is a bit like examining his own entrails, but it must be done.

The fact that a writer's style is so intimate a part of his deepest personality is doubly a handicap. The writer asked to question his own style is being asked to question his own inner being, which is nothing any of us do eagerly. The colleague asked to question a friend's style will more often than not decide to keep the friend rather than improve the friend's manuscript. Harsh words about grammar are one thing, harsh words about literary taste and judgment quite another.

Eagerly or not, the writer must do it for himself. It will not be a question of removing his own personality from the manuscript. That might be the worst error of all, for what will be left are words devoid of animation and an impression that the writer himself had no particular interest in what he was writing. (Doctoral dissertations generally read that way.) It is excess that must be sought out and removed, and not individuality; not style itself, but a surfeit of style, up to and beyond the point where it stifles the content of the document and calls attention to nothing except itself.

The writer who is enamored of his own style has no means of regarding it as critically as it must be regarded. Only the writer who has healthy doubts can familiarize himself with the manner in which he writes, and subsequently carry those healthy doubts into the process of revision. Taken all in all, it is much like jogging: not much fun in itself, but after it is over you are rather pleased with yourself.

Only an extremely disciplined writer, if such there be, can keep stylistic excess out of his manuscript. It is the way he naturally writes, or more properly one of the ways, for he is likely to be in command of more styles than one. To think about a natural act while performing that act is disabling; it brings two portions of the central nervous system into conflict with each other and they both misbehave. Far better to write naturally, and take time later to assure that you have written well.

Having been familiar with my own prose for a good many years, I believe myself capable of cataloguing the excesses which will always be found in my finished manuscript. Please note that the sentence you have just read is carefully qualified. Whether I am indeed capable is a question I cannot answer. I can only testify to my belief.

To begin with . . . and there is one of the excesses right there. My paragraphs almost always begin with a connective phrase of some kind or another, contributing nothing at all to the substance of what I have to say but acting as merely a mechanical link between the paragraph just concluded and the paragraph about to begin. There are times when the device is useful, for it gives a flow which is otherwise lacking, and makes a narrative easier to read. But if the flow is naturally there, as much of the time it will be, the mechanical linkage merely clanks, and in time it becomes wearisome.

That same paragraph carries a related excess: the overemployment of the parenthetical clause. Little is added to what I was attempting to say by the words "as much of the time it will be"; the thought is gratuitous, and slows down the reader for no good reason.

Finally, so far as structural sins are concerned, writing at speed I am inclined to begin sentences with phrases such as "It is" or "There is" or other flabby constructions. It is a common fault, and if I were not bent here upon preserving the scene of the crime, this very sentence would be revised to read "The fault is common."

The attentive among you will notice the tendency toward self-parody in this very passage. Each of the preceding three paragraphs began with a mechanical linkage to the prior paragraph. I am debarred by the nature of what I am doing just now from revising them, but be assured that under normal circumstances one or two of them would go.

But now on to more serious matters, of which facetiousness is one. I happen to be a person who is easily amused, and who finds mild amusement in amusing others. As a consequence, I tend to write facetiously, which is all very well when the reader is amused and extremely irritating when he is not. The nature of facetiousness is such that one man will chuckle where another will be wearied, and that with some frequency the only man who chuckles is the author of the facetious remark. It is a dangerous game. My revised manuscript is never as facetious as the draft, but I suspect that those who are my friends would wish it less facetious still.

The facetiousness perhaps serves my purposes best when I abandon it. It is intended to convey an air of lightness to what I am writing, and as a consequence on those occasions when the facetiousness drops away entirely it is clear that I am being as serious about something or other as I know how to be. It provides a contrast that would otherwise be missing. That helps me considerably when I call upon myself to justify its employment; I am not sure it persuades others. I am painfully aware that what I intend as lightness can quickly degenerate into a kind of snickering, which I like even less in myself than I like it in others.

Facetiousness also plays a part in a conscious attempt to introduce into every paragraph I write some element that will startle the reader, if only slightly. The stimulus may be the novelty of an idea, the incongruity of my choice of words, a mild impropriety, the calculated introduction of some personal idiosyncrasy—or facetiousness, which is introduced most often when I am about to be most serious. That element of my writing style is intended to help keep the reader awake, and if possible to persuade him that he can survive without switching on television for his evening fix. I am utterly convinced that it is a style worth cultivating, and equally convinced that it can easily go over the edge. I do my best to keep it under control, by being extremely alert to the danger when I revise, but I am certain that from time to time it escapes me.

I write allusively, which is not to everyone's taste. The allusions are natural, and come to mind without prompting of any kind when I write; I have no copy of <u>Bartlett</u> or the *Encyclopaedia Britannica* at my side. When I noted, some pages back, that it is no sin for a man to labor at his vocation, I did so because those were the words that came first to mind. I did not preface those words with "As Falstaff said . . . " because that is patronizing, and I have already counseled courtesy.

As a general matter, those who recognize the allusion will be rather pleased and in some instances self-satisfied, which serves my larger purposes. Those who do not recognize it to be an allusion will be unaffected as long as I am careful to keep the substance of my allusion appropriate. That leaves a few who know I have made an allusion but do not know just what I am alluding to; they are likely to be extremely annoyed. They are indeed few, and as a general practice I take the risk. But I know it to be an excess, and from time to time I remove an allusion, reluctantly.

A certain kind of parallelism can be found throughout. Almost always it takes the same form: an abstract statement is followed immediately by a concrete restatement. Thus in an earlier chapter, having asserted that a single word can constitute a sentence, I immediately added: " 'Stop!' is a sentence." That has become a part of my style and it is perhaps more studied than some of the other aspects, for I consider it a good habit and I think it adds to lucidity. Frank Loesser once pointed out to me three lines in one of his lyrics, which ran, as I remember them:

> thru the harbor and up to the quay,
> and there she stands, waiting for me,
> With a welcome so warm and so gay . . .

"I've fixed it so it doesn't matter how the singer thinks 'quay' is pronounced," he said. I use parallelism for the same sort of reason; the reader is bound to absorb the statement in one of the two forms, as his own mind best works.

Finally, I tend to employ irony: statements which convey one meaning and imply another, often opposite, meaning. Irony, when it is properly employed, intimates a kind of amiable conspiracy between writer and reader, and a covert understanding between them that others may not share; it couples people in a friendly sort of way. It is also extremely tiresome when it is overused.

Those, I believe, are the areas in which, as far as I can tell, I am most prone to excess. Other writers have other lists; I have listed my own because I know my own best. They are all present in this book, because no matter how conscious I am of those excesses, and no matter how sedulously I seek them out, they do not announce their presence to me as loudly as they do to others. It is not the habits per se but their excessive appearance—only mildly excessive when the final version appears—that enables those who are familiar with my writing to identify me as author even when the name is concealed.

I should add that although the list is as complete as I can make it, any reader will no doubt be happy to augment it. I am no better than the next man in seeing the mote in my own eye.

I am neither proud of those characteristics, or habits, or whatever they might be called, nor ashamed. They are my style. When I write with utmost gravity, the facetiousness is subdued or even concealed except perhaps from those who are privy to an allusion of some sort that most readers will not perceive. But it is still there. The paragraphs always tend to link; some of the parentheses survive the revision. The style is less and less marked as I revise, but it is still my style, and I have no desire to bleach it out entirely.

I perceive my style when I revise, or try very hard to perceive it, and I edit as I see fit. I am obliged to use my own judgment, and I do so with considerable confidence, thereby sparing myself a certain amount of agony and subsequent nervous breakdown. At the same time, I am conscious that I bear the responsibility for lapses.

Strunk and White have pointed out one element of style which may very well be common among all writers, and which I suspect to be associated with an intoxication at the sight and sound of one's own words. They express it in the form of a brief injunction: "Kill your darlings." I consider it to be the wisest single remark ever made about expository writing.

Every now and then, a writer engaged in revision will come across words which say exactly what he wishes to say in the most striking of all possible fashions, being at once wise, apt, witty, melodic, persuasive, ingenious and extremely moral. When anything of that sort occurs, the writer is duty bound to strike those words out. Ruthlessly. Regretfully, perhaps, but ruthlessly.

The point is simple enough. Words, sentences, paragraphs calling that much attention to themselves are not doing the job they are intended to do; indeed, they interfere with it. While the reader is paying them due reverence, he is likely to ignore the message they were meant to convey.

The "darling" is simply another kind of excess. Rare, to be sure, and a good deal more subtle, but excessive all the same. Mourn its loss, if you will, or treasure it in a scrapbook, but rend it from the corpus of your published works. Shed a tear only if you must.

(Oddly enough, there is an analogy in radio and television. Commercial messages brilliantly conceived and produced are in some instances admired and even sought out: some of the most memorable have been certain Bob and Ray commercials and the Mike Nichols–Elaine May commercials. The trouble, in both those instances and in others, was that although listeners and viewers reveled in the advertisements, they were rarely able to recall exactly what was being advertised.)

In all this there is an attractive symmetry. The manuscript itself is the object that is being produced, but the heart of the manuscript is to be found in the two activities that bracket it: the outline at the beginning, the revision at the end. The revision, simply because it sums up all that went before, is by far the more important of the two, and at the same time also the more tedious. (Lord, you should have seen that sentence before I got back to it!) The word processor has relieved it of almost all its tedium. An entire manuscript can be rearranged with a few commands; major alterations do not impose major retyping; repeated revision can be performed on legible hard copy.

That vast expanse of tedium made it tempting, once, to break off revising when there was still revising to do. The writer no longer has that excuse. Published writing should be better than ever.

Chapter Fifteen

Home at Last

Another damned, thick, square book! Always
scribble, scribble, scribble! Eh! Mr. Gibbon?

> DUKE OF GLOUCESTER, upon receiving from Edward
> Gibbon Volume II of The Decline and Fall of the
> Roman Empire

OVER the last several chapters I have chosen the odd course of
writing about what I am writing, and in the process lost some of
the generality with which I proposed initially to address my subject. The book, after all, is the least usual form assumed by expository writing, and not really representative of the genre as a whole.
I shall revert to the use of the word *document* in dealing with the
species; the book is simply one of many genera, and scarcely the
most populous. What is more, the book is at one extreme of the
range, with daily journalism and the ancient art of letter-writing
at the other.

Along the entirety of the range, the most fundamental distinction is between *mine* and *thine*. The book is very much the prop-
erty of the writer, whoever may chance to hold the copyright. For
the most part, the final form that is assumed by the book is determined by the writer, or by those to whom he has assigned the
privilege. The speech, on the other hand, belongs to the man who

delivers it and not the man who prepares it. The speaker chooses the writer and must approve the product. No writer worth his salt ever abandons his responsibilities entirely, but he must negotiate (or withdraw), for the power to command lies in other hands.

Perversely enough, writing for which the author does not hold the ultimate responsibility turns out much of the time to be the more responsible. To write in the name of an institution, or less frequently an individual, that the writer holds in high respect brings a great deal of discipline to the act. I have spoken at length of the excesses to which the writer is prone. He will never take greater pains to suppress them than when he is aware that they will be regarded not as his own excesses but as the excesses of some other person or some institution for which he cares. For similar reasons, he will be less likely to cut corners, less likely to manipulate, less likely to shrug off the constituency that might require considerable extra effort.

Periodical journalism degenerated seriously when it became the practice to reward the journalist almost automatically with his by-line. The best journals today are those few, such as The Economist, which have stubbornly insisted in all but exceptional circumstances that their reports are the reports of the journal itself and not of the correspondents who produced them. The deficiencies of television journalism are to a great extent a consequence of the fact that the institutional shield cannot be interposed even if there should be the will to do so.

A distinction that runs parallel much of the time with *mine* and *thine* is the distinction between restricted and unrestricted circulation. I am not referring to the odd practices of the military, or of government in general, but to quite ordinary considerations that govern ordinary social practices. Unless you happen to be Horace Walpole, the letter you write me is intended for my eyes alone, and is both written and read with that in mind. The report to his superior by a member of the staff has the same characteristic. The great bulk of expository writing is restricted, in that sense, to no more than a few readers; relatively little expository writing is published, or written in contemplation of a wide audience.

When the audience is more than a very few the document will almost inevitably be edited. The distinction between editing and what I have been calling *revision* is important enough to warrant the name of its own, although the two acts appear quite similar on the surface. In revision, the writer is attempting to meet standards that he himself establishes, although they may be standards powerfully affected by the nature of the audience he conceives himself to be addressing. The editor is an intervener, placed between the writer and the audience. When the writer remains in control of his manuscript, as is the case with most books, the first loyalty of the good editor in the good publishing house is to the writer, but he performs it in the light of his own knowledge and his own experience. If the writer has gone to a bad editor or a bad publishing house, and remains so associated, he has in fact lost control of his document, whether he knows it or not.

Wherever the document has been from the outset beyond the control of the writer, the nature of the editing will generally be a consequence of the status of the writer, and of the persistence he brings to the task of monitoring it. A willful and contemptuous superior could make hash of the King James Bible, and will generally make hash of anything else that comes within his reach. It serves no purpose to draw oneself up to one's full height and demand that the writer's name be removed from the document, since it was not going to be there in the first place. The writer is often tempted to snap "Keep your goddam money," but after a lapse of time measurable only by extremely refined methods he will always fight it off.

A kept writer is in the most favorable position when he is being edited by committee. In one instance I myself negotiated a long report almost word by word through a recalcitrant commission, playing one member off against another, and brought it through very nearly unscathed. It is not easy, but it can be done. If the writer is extremely adept and lucky, the committee itself will not be aware it is happening, and he will thus enjoy the great satisfaction of hearing the members congratulate each other on the immensity of their own writing skills. Oddly enough, it is a great satisfaction, but very much a satisfaction of its own sort, of which it is possible to have too much.

The writer bound for publication under his own name and in his own right, whether in a periodical, hard cover or soft cover, enjoys an entirely different relationship with his editor. So far as I am aware, no editor is an absolute cretin, and in the absence of information to the contrary I shall assume that to be a fact. I can then assert categorically that editing helps, and generally helps a great deal.

At the extreme, which is to be found wherever there is time pressure, as in daily newspapers and news magazines, the editing is dictatorial. Copy handed in at 9:00 P.M. which must reach the composing room at 9:30, even when it is handed in by computer, provides no time for courtly conversation over a glass of sherry. Gross misunderstandings between writer and copyreaders inevitably occur, and when they can be corrected between editions are generally patched up amiably. I have been long removed from the city room, but I suspect that it continues to be true that the journalist who quarrels with the men on the rim is almost invariably a very bad journalist. Grumbling, of course, is permitted, if not encouraged. It should not be carried too far, for all newspaper copyreaders have hemorrhoids and lean toward irascibility when they dare lean at all.

The editor brings a perspective to a writer's work that is useful simply because it is different from that of the writer himself. His words are not measured by considerations of either friendship or hostility. If he is a good editor, he has standards of his own which a writer will be able to respect. He also has a craft of his own, and if there are anything less than grave differences between a writer and his editor the chances are that the editor is right. And the good editor, finally, has a commitment to what he is editing that is no less serious than that of the man who wrote it; like the writer himself, the editor is doing the very best he can.

I myself fight tooth and nail with editors, but only over trifles.

The editor who corrects my grammar is in for a battle, since as far as I am concerned my grammar is always exactly correct and inviolable just as it is, and damn the consequences. At the same time, as soon as I have managed to drive that point home I cease to care about the matter entirely, and the editor can do as he pleases. About more serious matters I generally assume the editor is right. If he questions the lucidity of anything at all that I have written, he is absolutely correct by definition, although I may not agree at all with the manner in which he proposes to repair the damage.

The degree to which editing is a collaborative undertaking is likely to be governed by the nature of the subsequent manufacturing process, when there is one. Time pressure, as I have said, plays a large part. But however the editing is conducted, for the writer it marks the end of his travail. Proofs, if they come to him, are no more than a tedious tidying, like filing his notes or in my case moving them to where the trash man will find them. A writer who makes his final revisions in proof is not loved even if he is willing to pay the costs. After editing comes the finished product, although the lapse of time that occasionally intervenes stimulates the suspicion that someone somewhere must be doing something.

That finished product is the most reassuring aspect of the entire enterprise. It is extraordinary how much better it is than the manuscript it purports to reproduce. It looks better, of course, but some kind of necromancy has made the writing sharper, the logic more commanding, the general tone more seductive, and at the extreme even some of the facetiousness possesses a faint glint. It is enough to make a man try again.

I have been so intent upon those documents which eventuate in print or the equivalent that aside from an occasional reference to speech-writing I have ignored the many others. There are several fields of endeavor in which the written word plays an important part, although the end product is not the written word as it has been considered here.

Writing for television or the films is of course for the most part what I have been calling *creative* writing, although in both media there are productions called *documentaries* which are in modes crudely equivalent to expository writing or which pretend to be. In the early stages of preparing for either—the preproduction phases, as they are called—the task of the writer is very much like that of the ordinary expository writer, at least up to the point at which some kind of outline is beginning to take shape. Sooner or later, however, and in general the sooner the better, he must begin to take the picture into account, and his later outlines will refer to the camera and its ways at least as much as to the accompanying words, if any.

The words he will write intending their inclusion in the final product will of course be in the fashion of the spoken word rather than the written word, and even more narrowly may be calculated to reflect speech patterns of those who will utter them; other words will be calculated to stimulate a very particular kind of performance. Writing for Carl Sagan can scarcely be the same as writing for John Houseman (and aside from the money involved, neither is fit occupation for a grown man; my biases are showing). The whole process has a nature of its own, and its consideration would require a book of its own, of which I am qualified to write only a part although I have put in time, I have put in time.

It need hardly be said that the writer of such prose is not for a single moment in control. In the world of television and the world of the motion picture, his work is central to the entire enterprise, but the moment it leaves his hand a horde descends upon it and makes of it what they will. To be quite fair about it, they may be more talented in their own domains than the writer in his, but that is quite another matter. It is very hard work for a writer, and as one of them once remarked, "He works his fingers to the bone, and what does he get for it? Money!" That was Samuel Hoffenstein, who sublimated his frustration by contemplating his salary and writing very good light verse.

Something very much the same can be said about writing for radio, assuming that anyone actually <u>is</u> writing for radio; there is very little evidence and it has been many many years since I was in a position to know. There wasn't very much then, either. That writing, too, is quickly wrested from the writer and, in his terms, debased. In his case, the money is not all that good, either.

As for writing for advertising, it is an extraordinary skill in the hands of a few of its practitioners, like making pottery, and it does employ a distinct variety of the written word, but for the life of me I cannot think of anything else to say about it and do not propose to try.

What I have said in these last few paragraphs is clearly deprecatory, but I feel no need to apologize. At every level of their craft except perhaps the very pinnacles, those writers are a good deal more handsomely paid than garden-variety expository writers at the equivalent level. We balance it up by deprecating, and generally by living longer. It would be nice, though, to drive a Mercedes.

The distinction made earlier between the willing and the unwilling writer becomes useful again. They constitute two quite different types, and the rewards they derive from the practice of expository writing are also likely to be quite different.

The willing writer, more often than not, is likely to begin as an aspiring creative writer only to learn better with time, just as the professor of music appreciation is likely to begin as an aspiring concert pianist or something of the kind. The creator's talents are a good deal more rare than the craftsman's talents, which is perhaps all for the best, for we would otherwise be inundated by creativeness and all be most uncomfortable as a consequence. More soberly, a talent is creative only when it transcends the ordinary, and it takes no master statistician to recognize that there are no circumstances in which most of us can exceed the median.

The aspirant decides thereafter to make writing his career, or a significant part of his career, because it suits his temperament and he is more comfortable, by and large, with the environment within which writing casts him than within most of the practical

alternatives. That usually signifies that he is a somewhat introspective character who would rather think about things in general
than build bridges, wrestle, or order people about. He may even
sense, or learn, that he is extremely uncomfortable when he so
much as contemplates those sorts of activities.

For those of us so constituted (and I count myself among them)
it is a pleasant and a comfortable life. The craft is for them not
distressfully hard to learn or they would not be willing writers in
the first place. It is a quite respectable occupation, even so far as
to be held in well-controlled awe by those who *must* write and find
it difficult. The pay, as I have said, is ample if not stupendous, and
the working conditions are somewhere between healthy and unhealthy: they do not build the healthy body enjoyed by the life-
guard or the marathon hero, but neither are they positively lethal.
The work is solitary, for the most part, and despite the word
processor it still includes long patches of tedium, but it also provides a delight that seems part of the human condition: when a
task is finished, an object has been produced that can be held in
the hand and waved at the foe.

And finally, the writer can hope to leave his mark. He may after
all possess those special qualities that enable him from time to time
to achieve artistry, possibly when he expects it least. More often,
the imprint is not so readily recognized. In one restricted form it
was described superbly by John Maynard Keynes, himself a writer
of great talent who made his own mark by exactly the means he
describes, although his adjectives do not apply:

> Practical men, who believe themselves to be quite exempt from
> any intellectual influences, are usually the slaves of some defunct
> economist. Madmen in authority, who hear voices in the air, are
> distilling their frenzy from some academic scribbler of a few
> years back.

I have already quoted Jerrold Zacharias's more colorful version:
the man who holds the chalk runs the meeting. Still another quotation is relevant, although it emphasizes another aspect of the pro-

cess: "It is possible to do something," said A. Lawrence Lowell, "or to get credit for it, but not both."

All in all, it can be quite a good life.

As matters stand, most of the rewards enjoyed by the willing writer are not shared by the unwilling writer. Whatever his principal concerns may be, he has discovered to his dismay that a large part of his time is spent "pushing pieces of information about," many of which he must himself create or revise.

He does not enjoy it. For that there may be a good many reasons, but one is evident. If he is a person of any general competence, he has to be aware that he writes badly, and competent people do not enjoy the sense of having executed badly. Much writing he can assign to others, the willing or unwilling writers, but whether he is conscious of the fact or not, the power of the written word is such that assigning the task means assigning a certain amount of his authority, and deep down he is likely to know it. He risks also being betrayed in a fashion he does not quite understand. It is only right that he should be uncomfortable.

If the ordinary craft of expository writing were accessible to no more than a favored few, it would be enough to say that there exists an unfortunate state of affairs and let it go at that. It would simply be another fact, and we would all face up to living with it. I believe that the craft of competent expository writing can be taught. I believe that there is compelling evidence that it is not now being taught. And I believe firmly that it is within the power of the educational system to teach it, and even teach it well.

And to that subject I now propose to turn.

Chapter Sixteen

Learning

> Thou hast most traitorously corrupted the
> youth of the realm in erecting a grammar
> school; and . . . thou hast caused printing
> to be used; and, contrary to the king, his crown,
> and dignity, thou hast built a paper mill.
>
> WILLIAM SHAKESPEARE, Henry VI, Part II

UNTIL NOW I have been writing of matters about which I can perhaps assert a certain amount of authority, and certainly a good deal of experience. I shall now abandon my sheltered harbor and venture forth on strange seas. I have in the past submitted myself to the ministrations of educators, and dealt with them in other ways, but I have never been one of them. I do not have scholarly acquaintance with the mysteries over which they preside; neither have I faced a class of eager students or of any other kind of students. In short, I am grossly unprepared for what I am about to write, and I do not even possess the grace to be apologetic about it.

To begin with, two strong statements. First, an egalitarian educational system is not an educational system at all but more nearly a program for social reform. Second, the teaching of creative writing in the schools should be suppressed until at least the college years, and conceived thereafter as an enterprise distinct from the teaching of expository writing.

Now that I have your attention, I can concede that both statements, and particularly the latter, call for qualification, which I intend to provide. Even qualified, I do not expect that they will make me many friends, but I am not young any more and no longer expect to make new friends. The old ones, fortunately, seem to be hanging on.

Students do not enter the educational stream on equal terms. Even when they are five or six years old, differences among them have begun to emerge. There are those who are better coordinated than others, or handle language more easily, or manipulate objects more skillfully, or are more inquiring or more obedient. Some of that is probably innate and some a consequence of early environment; the tangle between the two is not that easily resolved.

The process of education, if it is not deliberately thwarted, accentuates those differences. If John, who is modestly proficient at finger painting, and Joe, who is slightly less proficient, enter kindergarten together, and if the kindergarten makes an honest attempt to teach finger painting, they will both move forward to the first grade in possession of improved finger painting skills, but the odds are that the gap between them will have widened. The odds also favor more of the same; if they study finger painting in the first and second grades the difference between them will widen still further, and by the time they matriculate at the California Institute of Finger Painting they are really no longer engaging in the same activity, although it may go by the same name.

If the purpose of the entire exercise is to create the most able finger painters—and that is an extremely big *if*—clearly somewhere along the line Joe should have been told to get out of the way. The shortage of skilled teachers of finger painting is generally acknowledged, and the financial resources required are hard to come by. However sincere Joe's urge to excel in finger painting, he is <u>in that respect</u> certainly a bad risk, and a stupid investment if the society believes it needs superior finger painters.

In those fields in which the development of high skills is conceded to be of great importance, the whole process is designed to get Joe out of the way as expeditiously as possible, and to encourage John. Boys who show promise in Little League baseball will be directed to a high school proud of its baseball prowess, if such a high school exists in the neighborhood; if it does not, his parents may be encouraged to move to a neighborhood where it does exist. All those boys arrive at high school showing great promise; they study baseball, with no more tolerance for fripperies than the law demands—but half of them do not make the team.

The half that does make it thereupon proceeds to a college which concentrates much of its attention on baseball. They are paid to attend that college, and little energy is wasted on the pretense that they are learning anything but baseball. Again they arrive with only a shadow of difference in their skills; again only a few make the team. After college the process continues for several years, up the ladder of the minor leagues, until a relative handful are admitted to postgraduate work with a major-league team. The thousands who began the process have been winnowed down to a few dozen at most, and still the differentiation continues; in the end only a handful win the accolade: they have become major leaguers, sign five-year contracts for $15 million, and immediately begin to let their skills deteriorate.

What I have described takes place only because baseball is perceived to be a matter of national importance and an educational system is brought into being that meets its needs. The high schools and colleges that engage in it act as educational institutions, so far as athletes are concerned. It is not a decision that is forced upon them; they can, if they wish, behave as a certain kind of social institution instead (as most do), in which case they organize in a different fashion. Or they may mix the two, as so very many do: they are educational institutions when they deal with athletes, and social institutions otherwise.

Of course, in a larger sense any educational system is a social institution. Education is itself a social need which that system is intended to satisfy. But education is only one of many social needs, and a system which calls itself educational but devotes its principal attention to those other needs, however important those other needs may be, has lost its way. It is not at all a question of importance. There may well be a national consensus that welfare programs take precedence over educational programs. If so, the nation should order its affairs so that it possesses a good, small educational system and a good, large welfare system, and so that the best-supported and best-staffed institutions within the good, small educational system be those which educate people to manage good, large welfare systems.

A good many people find such conclusions impalatable. A certain number of half-digested statements are hammered into all of us almost as soon as our language begins to make sense to us. We are informed that all men are created equal, and that a man is presumed innocent until found guilty, each of which is palpably untrue. The latter is a most necessary legal presumption; the law is obliged to <u>act</u> as if the suspect is guilty until he is <u>pronounced</u> guilty, but there are any number of instances in which no sane man would doubt his guilt. The equality with which we are endowed at birth is at best primarily a political equality, and the decision to confer it, a political decision. I support both the legal presumption and the political decision with all my heart and all my head. But language is likely to say more, or less, than it means when no conscious thought is applied to it, especially when its message can be made to conform with a view of affairs as they ought to be rather than as they are.

The handicaps confronting some people within any educational system are manifestly unfair. A part of the problem has been stated most acutely by a British economist, P. J. D. Wiles, who wrote: "Parental example and pressure, and a quiet study room at home, are indispensable to forming in the child the all-important <u>will</u> to be educated." (A generality, of course, and to be taken as such, but a very hard fact for a large number of people.) In certain respects, it goes even farther than Wiles suggests: it is most improbable that a person reared in an environment within which the native language is badly mauled will ever become proficient in the use of language. That is not fair at all, but there it is.

I am not suggesting that any person should be deprived of educational opportunities. I maintain only that the educational system which best serves all who enter is a severely tracked system which allows the maximum of mobility between tracks. If society wishes the services of highly educated men and women it must put up with an educational system of which some portion is designed maximally for those most likely to benefit from it. That is exactly the way the system is designed for athletes, and it works extremely well. It should be designed that way for all, including—almost in passing—those of high intellectual capacity. A few institutions of higher education, and a very few public schools, meet the needs of those who can benefit from high learning; most do not. Fewer still meet the needs of all the rest unless, as I have said, they are athletes.

It is really "the rest," and not the intellectual, that concerns me. One way or another the intellectual will cope; it is society that suffers, more than the man himself, if his skills are not as sharply honed as they might be. I am a good deal more troubled by those who are obliged to pass through an educational system that counterfeits the life of the mind. Such a system deprives the individual of his satisfactions and the society of his services, and appears to me to make no sense at all. For the most part, that is the system we have.

I may appear to have set off on a jog across country. Yet I am still dealing with the written word, and I am not far from the stable even now.

Nominally the school system does not stint in its efforts to teach the young reading and writing. The process begins almost as soon as the child enters the system, encouraging him to develop the motor control necessary to inscribe words on paper, and to recognize either the letters that constitute the alphabet or selected words in which those letters appear. There was once a certain amount of controversy about reading, with one school of thought advocating the old-fashioned alphabetic route and the other moving to phonics, by which was meant word recognition. For all I know, the controversy may still smolder somewhere in the underbrush of the schools of education. Historically, of course, the word certainly came first, but history has never been much of a guide in developing educational patterns or we would all learn to drive by reading James Watts's blueprints. Either way, the kids learned to sort it out, and the difference in the approaches was nothing more than a parochial quarrel among the scholarly and the semi-scholarly.

Until fairly recently, an honest attempt to teach reading and writing continued through all the years of precollege education, and here and there it reappears from time to time. But in many systems the secondary student is given the opportunity to play with film or, I suppose, television tape instead, and in others the whole enterprise is conducted in a spirit of hopelessness. College, these days, is where serious attempts to teach writing take place, without very much success, and then only the very best colleges.

I see no need to argue the point that such a state of affairs is shocking, since no one who has read this far is likely to feel otherwise unless he is reading on in order to stimulate his bile, in which case argument is not likely to matter. In my own view, clearly biased by the nature of my own predilections, all that incapacity is a crime or perhaps, as Talleyrand is said to have remarked in other circumstances, worse than a crime: a mistake!

There are those who believe it to be something else again: the inevitable consequence of the insinuation of television into the very marrow of our bones. We discovered a few years ago, during the expeditions of inquiry to which I have already referred, that many and perhaps even most teachers have adopted that view, citing television and cognate activities as a kind of impotency principle, and classifying any serious attempt to teach old-fashioned literacy as still one more search for a perpetual-motion machine.

My faith is somewhat different. I do believe it to be unlikely that any teacher, however dedicated, can teach any student, however able, the mysteries of creative writing, although a first-rate teacher may be able to help a first-rate student learn. I believe also that any student, within limits, can be taught expository writing and I feel confident that I can even state the limits: he will be able to write approximately as well as he thinks. A few will write better than that, but not very much better; some will write worse, but not necessarily very much worse.

That faith, coupled with my own sadly jaundiced views on broader matters, leads me to believe that a great many people, simply because they do not think coherently, will never learn to write. I do not for one moment believe that they are inferior because they do not think in that very special kind of way, any more than I believe an intellectual to be superior because he does. I happen to feel more comfortable with the intellectual, by and large, but that is a statement about *me* and has no further field of reference. What is more, I insist that the educational system owes every individual the best education it can provide him. In some very extreme circumstances that may mean no education at all; for the rest of us it means the most appropriate education, which in turn means as surely as night follows day some kind of tracking.

In all this it is possible to detect snobbery if one goes to a good deal of trouble to do so. I do not believe a fair-minded person would find it, although he might very well object on other grounds. I would far rather spend my time with some kinds of people than with other kinds, but it is not because I believe them to be superior. They <u>are</u> different, and that is readily detectable. Whether or not they are "better," and indeed whether to say they are "better" carries any real meaning, are matters I would find it very difficult to deal with. I do know there are people who make quite different choices, and it seems to me that they have the same

privileges I have. Many years ago, when automobile air-condition-
ers were rather primitive, I drove across the southwestern desert
with one of the kind that hung on the window of the car, and on
arriving in Salt Lake City asked a friend if he "could use an air-
conditioner." Somewhat warily, I thought, he replied, "Under
what circumstances?" A most sensible question, not asked nearly
often enough.

During all the years of early education, once the sheer mechanics have been conveyed in some rudimentary form, writing is
taught in association with reading, and both are taught in the
broad context of both creative and expository writing. There is
really very little that can be said about creative writing that is
much more than gushing, at least until the student has gained
considerable maturity. Creative writing is therefore not easily
handled. A good deal of what is read in the upper grades is unmis-
takably creative writing, but a normal twelve-year-old reading
Julius Caesar is simply following orders, and might be just as well
served if he were put to reading road signs.

There is at the same time the assumption of a Platonic form of
the English Language, to use the language of earlier pages, and of
its uniform relevance to every aspect of writing. As a consequence, it is held that mastery of grammar and spelling and syntax
and punctuation, and a profound exploration of the paragraph,
will automatically make the student a spellbinder in any writing
mode he may choose, from lyric poetry to the unerring composition of laundry lists. All that is patent nonsense, and it is worth
wondering how it arises.

The most respectable justification for acting on those views lies
in what I would call an undeniable fact: the best writing in any
language, and the best literature in any language, is the kind that
I have been calling *creative.* In the circumstances of the school-
room the consequences seem clear enough. Surely the student
should read the very best. And surely he should learn the rules that
are uniformly agreed to govern the very best, since (against all the

evidence) the learned have been saying so for approximately a hundred and fifty years.

After that, the reasons are less defensible. It is very easy, for example, under the ground rules that apply, to assert confidently whether a given patch of spelling, or a foray into the thickets of grammar, is right or wrong. On the basis of judgments such as those, a student may be elevated to the head of the class, or relegated to the tail, or in those establishments backward enough to retain some of old-time brutality, even failed.

If the minatory eye is held firmly upon such questions as those, moreover, it becomes unnecessary to bother too much about what the student actually wrote. The hard fact that certain forms of writing, although by no means all, require the writer to make sense, may be given lip service, but to ask more of the teacher is to ask <u>him</u>—more likely, <u>her</u>—to make sense and to say what "*making sense*" means and implies. A tall order, particularly when most of those to whom the attention is being directed are too young to have advanced very far in that particular direction, and a certain number will never advance very far at all.

Finally, and perhaps most important of all, the emphasis on creative writing and the dismissal of any other kind is likely to reflect the predispositions of the teacher. Somewhere along the passage from first grade to higher education, teachers begin to be classified by specialty. The English teachers among them have chosen that field of endeavor not entirely of their own free will. More often than not, they are what I have chosen to call "willing writers." Like almost all such writers, themselves affected by their own educations, they have been encouraged to believe that they have talents as creative writers. A few turn to teaching as an interim measure, until the world discovers that they have those talents. Others know that they have been deceived and turn to teaching because it is what they believe they can do best, or somewhat more nobly hoping to create in their own students the talents they themselves seem to have lacked.

Those teachers are honestly and honorably doing what they

think best. The system as a whole supports them and parents, products of the system, rarely propose anything but more of the same. On it goes.

It is a comfort to have rules, for rules can be taught. Creative writing, unfortunately, has no rules worth talking about, or it may be that the rules are clear only to other creative writers. Expository writing, on the other hand, has a few very clear rules, comprehensible to the dullest among us. The first and most fundamental of all those rules is simple: Make yourself understood. Everything else is an elaboration of that fundamental rule, or is secondary.

I was told once of a teacher in a private secondary school, and consequently favored with manageably small classes, who developed what he called "the peanut butter method" of teaching expository writing to a first-year class. I do not believe the story for a moment, but I will tell it.

The first task assigned those students directed them to prepare a paper, length unspecified, entitled "How to Make a Peanut Butter Sandwich," to be handed in a few days thence. On the appointed day, the papers were delivered to the instructor, who promptly produced several jars of peanut butter and as many loaves of bread. Thereupon, grimly and ruthlessly, he went through paper after paper, proceeding exactly as each paper told him to, making "peanut butter sandwiches." At the end of the hour the classroom, the teacher's desk and the teacher himself were a welter of bread and jars and paper and peanut butter, but there was not so much as a single sandwich to be found. "Boys," he said to the class, "obviously we have work to do."

If any such exercise had taken place, it might very well have occurred to the students for the very first time what expository writing was all about. At the moment, clearly, it did not matter very much to their instructor how they had spelled "peanut butter"; he wanted only to be clear what they meant. He was concerned with what they wrote about peanut butter, which was enormously more consequential than the way they spelled it. I do not suggest that with his sticky demonstration the instructor's work was done; only that he and the class were on the right track, and that perhaps for the first time in their lives the members of the class realized why they were being asked to learn how to write. Papers called "How I Spent My Vacation" would not have been quite the same.

If it really happened, of course.

My insistence, a long way back, that the teaching of creative writing should be suppressed was deliberately provocative, but I do not intend to apologize for it. Making myself clear, however, is an obligation I cheerfully honor.

The notion of extracurricular activities is certainly familiar in the American educational system. I made far too much of athletics somewhere along the line; they are treated in most schools and for most students as extracurricular, and that treatment does not carry with it so much as a scintilla of disrespect. But I need not stress that point any longer, for I am sure that I have long since made it clear that whatever I may feel about creative writing cannot possibly be classed as disrespect.

I propose that creative writing be handled in the schools much as athletics are handled and on the whole a great deal more positively. The young student should be encouraged to write imaginatively, to make up stories, to experiment with verse—to <u>play</u> at writing in the very best sense of the word. The teacher should applaud the effort, make suggestions, express regret, and even give more active assistance when it is requested (which will be rare). I realize I am increasing the teacher's load, but I do not believe unreasonably so.

And the student should be urged to read creative literature as his fancy may direct; the teacher should be prepared with suggestions and the school with the books and magazines. It is exactly the obligation that ordinary schools recognize with respect to athletics, providing the field and the coach.

There is a difference, however, between athletics and creative writing. On the playing field at any time are athletes and those who are merely doing athletics. There is a certain amount of conflict between the two groups, but it is manageable. What is more important is that the conflict is largely spatial. The values that athletics carries for the amateur are the values of a sound body and the enjoyment of play. Those values, together with others I scarcely need specify, are present for the athlete as well. In the end, almost without exception, those who fancied themselves athletes will discover they are not anything of the sort, because they cannot hit curves or dive reflexively to the exact site of a batted ball. They will direct their attention to other matters, and the time they spent playing baseball will not interfere in any serious fashion, and may even have created in them the habit of healthy exercise. (Football may leave them with a lifetime of aches and pains, but that is another matter entirely.)

Writing is something else again. Unlike athletics, it has a place well within the curriculum because it represents something that all must achieve in some measure, amateur or professional, and that under existing conditions a very large number should learn to do reasonably well, in their own interests and in the interests of society. What they must learn is precisely expository writing, and not creative writing. And it is not only that the two are different. They fight each other. What is quite right in one kind of writing is quite wrong in the other.

Let me now, for clarity's sake, change the image without doing violence to the argument, and move abruptly from baseball to golf. The aspiring golfer and the aspiring creative writer, regarded with the cold eye of the statistician, are alike doomed to fail. The creative writer will find he cannot write; the golfer will realize that he is doomed to a lifetime of 85's, or 75's, or even 70's, none of which will do him much good. No great matter. The game still remains; he will play the game, and enjoy it, with some mild regret that he could not challenge Jack Nicklaus but no deep unhappiness because he never *did*.

Writing is not like that. For only a few people does writing, creative or expository, have any of the qualities of a game: the excitement of competition, the animal delight of winning. The student who becomes aware that his talents do not extend to creative writing does not give up only creative writing but may give up writing entirely, in part because it is associated in his mind with failure, and in part because he does not really know what it is; he was never taught. If he must write, he does so reluctantly, with foreboding, and not surprisingly, quite badly.

And one more factor is worth taking into consideration. The formal curriculum in creative writing does not accomplish anything at all that it purports to accomplish. It is intended to introduce the young to the noblest works of literature, but no introduction means very much unless both parties are willing to participate. Perhaps a few students are to be found, here and there, in whom that kind of reading habit is created in the school; I have never known one. If the literary bent comes from outside the individual at all, it is immeasurably more likely to come from the home, created by the habits of parents and their friends. That generalization applies as much to creative writing as to reading. But I am being far too kind. The marginal student, who might enjoy and understand good literature and might not, is far more likely to be repelled than attracted by any of the curricula I have seen, or many of the teachers I have met. As the nonce word has it, the curriculum is counterproductive.

It should not be necessary, but I suspect that I had best repeat that my complaint is against creative literature in the curriculum. I support creative literature in the schools with every bone in my body. Indeed, it is just because I myself love it so that I object so thoroughly to the damage done, in literature's name, within the schools, and quite unnecessarily.

Do not look upon me as a hard and inflexible antagonist of education as a whole. The ultraconservative critics of education look upon it as an institution intended to preserve society as it is, and oppose anything at all that suggests some other function. The ultraradicals look upon it as an institution intended to preserve an existing corrupt system, and would go even to the lengths of destroying it altogether. I hold neither view. If I am radical in any way at all, it is in believing that writing, and mathematics as well, are different in that each has a creative aspect and a utilitarian aspect, and that the two aspects do not coexist in comfort. If I am conservative, it is in believing that usefulness is not to be deplored, and that an educational system should encourage it wherever that may be appropriate.

My faith is that anyone who needs to write expository prose can learn to write expository prose. Not without a certain amount of pain, perhaps, but there is nothing out of the ordinary about that. I am not sure that I know exactly how to go about it, but I do have certain notions and I am willing to extend my neck. That is the next, and final, order of business.

Chapter Seventeen

In Conclusion

> I do not know which to prefer,
> The beauty of inflections
> Or the beauty of innuendos.
> The blackbird whistling
> Or just after.
>
> WALLACE STEVENS, "Thirteen Ways of Looking
> at a Blackbird"

To BEGIN WITH, something about the mechanics.

The youngster past his toddling prime and newly enrolled in the first grade is in no way to be envied. He faces many tasks, and one task he faces immediately has to do with writing. In my own days the task was accompanied by something I can only call savagery, the Palmer Method. Decades have come and gone, and I can still remember every detail. It was a form of calligraphy that I have never in my life known to be employed by any but elementary-school teachers, and generally not even by them outside the classroom.

To this day I remember my shock when I found that my fifth-grade teacher, an aged spinster of about twenty-nine named Miss Quinn, created capital *M*'s in a fashion never so much as mentioned by Mr., Mrs., or Miss Palmer. I was so entranced that I promptly began to emulate her, and for several weeks both of us managed to write capital *M*'s in a style that effectively concealed the fact that they were intended to be capital *M*'s or anything of the sort. I finally ceased; whether or not Miss Quinn ceased I cannot say.

I tell that story not out of nostalgia but to make the point that the association of patent nonsense with the pedagogy of the written word is no recent development. It seems to be constant over time, so I was not astonished some years back when my wife was gravely advised by a teacher in what is generally considered a first-rate school system that my older son, then eight, would stand no chance whatsoever of being admitted to college unless his penmanship improved, and would consequently be lost to honest society. He has indeed been lost to honest society—he is a practicing attorney—but his penmanship had nothing to do with it.

Writing legibly by hand is tedious and difficult. A few people manage it, but even they lapse into illegibility, or something very near, when they must write more than a few sentences. To make the problem more acute, the act of writing is a painfully slow transcription of thought, which itself moves extremely rapidly and is evanescent. There is every reason to advise the writer to get his words on paper as expeditiously as possible, which faces even the adult with Hobson's choice, for if he does choose to write fast he may succeed in getting his words on paper but he will not be able to read them.

Typing is not difficult to learn, and for the child is probably a good deal easier than writing since it involves considerably less fine muscle control. But this time the writer is betrayed in another part of his task. Editing by typewriter is, or has been, extremely difficult, and the temptation to scamp it is overwhelming.

Most of those who write a good deal combine the two methods, writing by machine and editing by hand. The combination is tedious and in some respects combines the worst of both worlds along with the best. For the child, faced with a great many problems in connection with writing and not yet quite knowing just why he is expected to do anything about them, the whole affair is likely to be seen as punishment, whether he is asked to tackle it by hand, or by machine, or both.

The dilemma, however, is exactly the sort of thing that is child's play for the computer, and it begins to appear that the computer, programmed to be quite literally child's play as a word processor, is tackling it. The notion of a children's computer is anything but new, since probably more than half of all computers are sold to be used playing Pac-Man or Star Wars or something else idiotic, by children ranging from five to upwards of thirty. A good deal more serious work for children was done by Papert and others at M.I.T., and the resulting computer language, LOGO, is now widely available. But as far as I know, the only direct attack upon early education in the written word is the work of The Bank Street School of Education in New York. The results, and beyond that what they seem to promise, I find staggering.

The Bank Street Writer, as the software is called, is now available. I am not making a case for it here, for a variety of reasons, of which the most important is that I believe it is in its earliest stages and will be improved, and that competitors are almost certain to put in an appearance with versions of their own, some of which may be considerably better. The Bank Street Writer is of interest for what I think it has clearly demonstrated.

First, children do not have to be taught to use it; they simply learn, just as they simply learn how to use crayons. Being children, they do not find the computer and all its associated paraphernalia mysterious; they were looking at television screens while they were still in the maternity ward. I would not be surprised if the crayon seemed a good deal more mysterious. In any case, the children sit down before it, and bang it around a bit, and when it responds by displaying letters they make it display more letters, and while it would be excessive to suggest that they immediately type out "The Tempest: Act I, Scene I" and get down to work, they really do begin to get organized quite on their own. It all seems so natural, which cannot be said of the Palmer Method.

The whole experiment is far too new to have yielded reliable results. Then, too, even moppets are no doubt subject to the Hawthorne Effect. It does appear, though, that at ten and eleven and twelve children write far more acceptably on such a machine than otherwise, and do so with less formal instruction. I must say that I would be astonished at any other result. The promise of such a development seems to me to be incalculable; I worry only that the educational establishment will fight the whole thing off.

If the establishment tries to do so, it will of course be abetted by those who think that hand calculators are immoral and these newer devices come not from Silicon Valley but from Hell itself. The benefits consequent upon multiplying, by hand, 59273 × 921046 and getting the wrong answer have always escaped me. The notion that a child should be forced to go through such exercises when it is clear that he will never do anything comparable during his adult life is no less than insane. The notion that he should be forced to write sustained messages by hand when far simpler means are available is more insane still. But the opposition will be there, and may overcome.

I hope not. The word processor might be the greatest single contribution of the computer to early education; I would even go so far as to suggest that it might be the only contribution. Let us pray, and while we are doing so encourage those who are capable of dealing with such matters to put their minds to work on the problem.

Before I leave this subject, I wish to muse aloud on a related matter. Few would deny a close linkage between reading and writing, and there would also be general agreement that only those who learn to read efficiently come to write efficiently: that reading is the prior accomplishment. Certainly a child does learn to read before he learns to write, although what he reads is "Exxon" and other such inspiring literature.

After all, however, children are small, disagreeable adults with very strong egos. I suspect that like adults what they would be most likely to enjoy reading is anything they themselves have written. The word processor not only makes that possible: it positively encourages it, and provides tidy printed pages for the purpose. I am suggesting, in short, that the contribution of the computer is as much to reading skills as to writing skills. One of these days Bank Street and those who follow may be able to tell us something about that.

Once the student has learned to deal with the mechanics of writing, with all the aid the word processor can provide, he must learn why he is being asked to write in the first place, and how to go about it. All I have been writing makes it clear that I believe he should be advised that he is being asked to write expository prose because he bloody well better know how, for his own good and that of his fellows. That means learning how expository prose is written, and writing some of it himself.

Everything in this book before I developed symptoms of megalomania in the last chapter and this one has been directed toward an understanding of how expository writers actually write. There has been an inescapable emphasis upon how I myself write, but I am typical of the breed and I know that differences between my procedures and those of my fellows are no more than differences of detail. The teaching of expository writing, like the teaching of any other craft, should introduce the student to those procedures, instill as much understanding as possible of the rationale that underlies them, demand the drill that will make them familiar and customary, and provide the supervision and correction that will make the drill serve its purposes.

The curriculum, accordingly, would begin at every stage with reading and outlining. The reading should be selected from expository writing of quality that deals with subjects in which the students themselves take a real interest. I have no illusions about the quality of the writing generally to be found in newspapers and periodicals, but there is a very large amount of it and some of it is bound to be good. Out of the great mass there is more than enough that deals with matters with which the young of this age or that are concerned: sports, rock-and-roll, television—it does not really matter what.

The outlining, initially, should deal with the reading matter that is being provided. The student should be asked to make an outline of what he has been assigned to read, and the several outlines exposed to the class as a whole, first for examination of the fidelity of the outline to its source, and second for some comprehension of why the outline from which the writer must have worked assumed the form that it did assume.

At some point, the students should begin preparing outlines of their own, and those outlines should be subjected to scrutiny. Sooner or later in the course of human events the class should reach the stage where a decent proportion of the students have mastered the outlining process to a degree commensurate with their own maturity. Only then should the class begin the task of converting their own outlines into expository prose. The goal of the exercise should be "make yourself understood." It should be noted, firmly but as very much a secondary matter, that a certain knowledge of syntax and spelling and other such matters is essential to being understood.

In all this I would expect the word processor to play a major role. As a simple matter of course, the student would learn how to spell, without fuss of any kind, from his word processor. Note that I do not suggest that the word processor would <u>teach</u> the student to spell, but that the student would <u>learn</u>. Any word-processing program worth its salt makes provision for a spelling checker, and it is not beyond the wit of man to design a spelling checker for the particular needs of the middle years of schooling or the subsequent years as they may be best defined. Such a checker calls attention to misspelled words and demands that they be corrected, which is exactly how any person learns to spell except in school.

It has been said of a well-known economist that if he doesn't <u>know</u> your telephone number he will be happy and indeed anxious to make an estimate. That is somewhat silly when telephone numbers are in question, but very sensible when it is a matter of spelling, as long as it concerns words in only your passive vocabulary or not in any of your vocabularies at all. Estimates are quite good enough, since you will not need the word when you write, and it will be spelled for you when you read. If by chance the word should become part of your active vocabulary, for any reason at all, it will be time enough then to find out how it is spelled. The word processor's spelling checker has the great merit that it helps you learn the spelling of words that you want to spell and ignores the rest, saving you a good deal of unnecessary exertion.

The word processor, in short, adheres to the normal, human method instead of imposing an artificial, mechanical, utterly unmotivating method of learning to spell.

The educational process I am here suggesting demands a good deal of writing, and consequently a great deal of reading by someone or other. That reading should be done primarily by the students themselves, and now again the word processor, along with the copying machine, is a necessity. The class as a whole should analyze first, under the guidance of its teachers, the outlines its members have submitted and later the resultant prose. This, too, is a human method of getting from here to there, made possible by obedient, rather stupid machines. (The book itself, so much an object of reverence and well worth it, is also the product of obedient, stupid machines.)

The role of the word processor in revision, which of course is an indispensable part of the process, scarcely needs any special attention. As an ordinary matter of course, no human being who possesses ordinary intelligence can use a computer for any purposes at all without being driven to revise up to the point of useful return and sometimes beyond. I have known otherwise normal people who, having completed the creation of a computer program which runs routinely in 2.5 seconds, thereupon devote a month of useful time to reducing its running time all the way down to 2.4 seconds. The urge toward elegance can be a ruination in more than writing.

The introduction of some form of tracking into the process is not anything that appears to require elucidation. At any rate, I am not going to attempt it here. Enough hackles have no doubt already been raised to threaten the general peace.

How all this would work I simply do not know, although obviously I have faith. At an absolute minimum, it would be better than what we have. But in one of his songs Tom Lehrer deposed as follows:

"Once the rockets are up, who cares where they come down? That's not my department," says Werner von Braun.

My sentiments exactly.

Although it wearies me, I know that I am obliged to reiterate that nothing I propose prevents a student from reading the collected works of John Keats, or the teacher from encouraging him to do so. Indeed, he is not even prevented from attempting to write an ostensible equivalent of the collected works of John Keats, or an equivalent that is something more than ostensible, although in the latter instance his odds would be far better if he were to devote his energies to interplanetary tourism. That, however, is his business and not yours, or mine, or the business of the educational system.

Indeed, I suspect that a familiarity with the workings of expository prose can only benefit the creative writer, as little as he may wish to choose expository prose as a medium in which to express himself. But I do not know enough about creative writing to begin making a persuasive case.

Other aspects of all this do not stimulate nearly as much temerity as I have been displaying until just now. Systematic general education carries with it an obligation to differentiate as it proceeds, and tracking is only a part of that obligation. During the early years the student is expected to learn a very little about almost anything he might reasonably understand; as he proceeds he is asked to learn a good deal more about a few things that society considers important; at the highest reaches of graduate education he concentrates his energies upon learning more and more about less and less. The sequence at its best is most efficient, but it is artifice, for the man himself does not readily subdivide that way, and neither does his universe, or the way his mind works.

Given the nature of expository writing, and the manner in which it must be mastered, it is perhaps necessary to conclude that it will be best learned not in a context of its own but in another context: the context of history, or political science, or even ichthyology or cookery or pure mathematics or what you will, so long as "what you will" has a structure and a significance of its own. To say that the aim of the expository writer is to make himself understood is to be extremely elliptical: his aim is to make himself understood about something.

Certainly the very best expository writing on science, for whatever audience you might name, has been achieved by scientists themselves and not by those who think of themselves as expository writers, and the equivalent statement can be made about all areas of knowledge in which it still remains possible for the expert to shake off the jargon of the mystery he happens to profess. But what the very best can achieve in any field carries no implications whatsoever for systematic education. The business of helping people learn in any advanced society is a very large business, occupying the attention of a very large portion of that society. Whenever a very large portion of society is engaged, most of that large portion will be mediocre or worse. (A friend of mine used to arouse angry cries of "Fascist" whenever he pointed out that most people are average or below average—I expect a similar judgment.) Any major institution that cannot get its job done by mediocre people is bound to fail. Like it or not, history teachers as a group will not teach expository writing, although some of the best of them no doubt will do so whatever the system, and heaven bless them.

Expository writing, in short, is going to be the responsibility of those who are responsible for teaching expository writing, and now once again, as so often, we are back to the way in which we choose to employ the language. I distinguish between *teaching* and *helping to learn,* although it is possible to consider them synonymous. Given the essential nature of the educational system, *teaching* is likely to be a disservice to the student who has a potential to be somewhat better than the average. I consider it an unexpected blessing that a large portion of society, much of which is itself mediocre or worse within the context of what it is doing, is suddenly and without conscious purpose creating machines that help people learn. A miracle, an honest miracle.

But wait. Here again I find myself obliged to say, as I have said before, "Here lie dragons."

I have made a case for the educational system that we possess, and I have made as good a case as I know how to make for severe tracking, and for the machine. But the case for tracking brings with it the obligation to test, and the nature and size of the educational system is such as to make it inadvisable to rely with any confidence upon the capacity of the system to test judiciously.

Even though we appear to have refused, as a society, to welcome tracking, we have gone to the machine for testing. The multiple-choice examination is such a machine, and gains much of its power and its practicality from its own employment of the computer, which is far more readily recognizable as a machine. The multiple-choice test removes the power of decision from the members of the educational society as a whole and turns it over to those conceived to be the most competent among them, aided by applied mathematicians and the scholars of cognition.

However angrily the opponents of multiple-choice testing may protest, it appears that the multiple-choice test works most satisfactorily over most of its range. I suspect that it never does justice to the very able, but on the whole one need not worry about the very able, for they generally take care of themselves. Indeed, they are almost certain to possess the special abilities necessary to defeat the multiple-choice test.

Unfortunately, however, within the portion of the range over which it is least successful lie the matters we are considering here.

All in all, multiple choice serves its purposes where its points of reference lie outside those whom it tests. To a first approximation —and no basic test goes farther—there is only one correct answer to the question "What is the speed of light?" and any number of incorrect answers from which the man who composes the examination may select any four he chooses. Any primitive machine permits the system to single out those who provided the correct answer, although it is true that the student a year or two ahead of his class might want to be able to ask "Under what circumstances?" Only if he was marked by the gods for a career in the law, however, would he check off the box for "1100 feet per second" and bring suit if it was marked wrong.

Expository writing, however, is a mode of thought, and thoughts are by no means external to those who think them. There is no uniquely correct sentence independent of what the writer is attempting to say and what the reader hears; there is an infinite number of correct sentences, each of them contingent. In the end, the correctness of my sentence is what you make it and whatever uniqueness it may possess is relative to that coupling at that time. A sentence can be called "best" when it conveys _my_ meaning to the largest possible number of _my_ readers, but that still does not make it "correct." In any case, I have no notion of how one would determine such an outcome by means of a multiple-choice test which offers five sentences to choose from, none of which I would be likely to write.

The multiple-choice test, accordingly, will be a test of the conventions that the educational system is obliged to impose upon the student for no other reason than the fact that his ability to memorize those conventions can indeed be tested. Give them their due: those who prepare the tests will work to the limits of their capacity, by no means negligible, to do better, but the nature of the task puts that forever beyond them. The only test of expository writing is expository writing and a respectable sample of readers, which cannot practically be achieved upon the required scale.

I have been foolhardy in these chapters, but I am not so fool-

hardy as to suggest that I know how this dilemma is to be overcome in general, although I might be able to suggest fashions in
which it might be handled in special situations. Obviously, a first-
rate teacher would be able to handle it with ease, but I have
forsworn the appeal to first-rate teachers although I know that a
good many exist. I wish I believed that a better computer could
do the job. If you follow one current line of thought down to the
end, you may come to the conclusion, as I do not, that the artificial-
intelligence fraternity already have a handhold on the problem.
That will cheer you, no doubt, but all the rest of us can do is go
on thinking or perhaps, like Miniver Cheevy, go on drinking.

An intermediate position, flecked with optimism, would be that
the current state of affairs is transient or could be made so. Teachers are not the victimizers but the victims, made so by their own
early education; most of them teach as they do because they are
quite naturally inclined to teach as they were taught, altering the
ornamentation a la mode but never questioning the durability of
the underlying fabric.

I suppose that must be my position, since I cannot very well
advocate change without some expectation that change can be
managed. Still, out of the corner of my eye I see the dragons.

I have said by this time all that I think I know about expository
writing, and some that I think I know about other matters more
or less prime to the occasion. I have also said a good deal that I do
not think I know but merely know I think, or try to think. Two
different states of mind entirely, although a verbal jungle.

Closed solutions to the problems I have tried to raise or illumi-
nate are out of the question, which is characteristic of most problems that arise in the real world. Since the solutions we are now
applying are not solutions at all, it is necessary to keep looking, and
that I have done.

I stand on the position with which I began. The issue is something more than current educational practices. There was a time
when the professional scribe dealt with the matter of expository

writing and nothing more was required, since there was not very much demand and most of that was frivolous. That time has passed.

"The question is which is to be master," wrote Lewis Carroll, "that's all." The remark has a deprecatory ring, but the underlying significance is not at all to be deprecated. One can be hardheaded and practical, and appeal only to the chilly fact that a great many people these days make their living in fashions which involve them directly with expository writing and allied activities, and garner material rewards determined in part upon the skill with which they manage those activities. Or one can aspire to profundity, and assert that greater affairs than that are at stake, and that in the kind of society we have the way we write and the way we read what others have written may affect a good deal more than material rewards. Long after Orwell's death we have reached the milepost that he planted, and at that milepost, you will recall, the first thing that went was language and the manner in which it was used. Everything else followed.

Our humanity begins with language and the manner in which we use it. For those who look to religion for wisdom, so says the Bible and I suspect so say all the Holy Books, for they tend to be the same. But wherever you choose to look, you will see something of the sort. It should certainly not be surprising that those who write say so, and most of the where you look turns out to be in the written word.

We who call ourselves *Homo sapiens* are masters of language and consequently slaves of language. It seems reasonable to suggest that we be aware of what language is, and how it is employed. To that end, this book is intended as a modest contribution, although the modesty may not always be as evident as it might be.

So be it.

Index

Permissions Acknowledgments

About the Author

Stephen White was born in Boston, attended Harvard College and wandered into journalism. He was successively science writer, editorial writer and roving European correspondent for the *New York Herald Tribune;* then European Editor and Assistant Managing Editor of *Look* magazine, thereafter abandoning journalism except for occasional forays into television for CBS News. His writing has since taken him here and there, including eight years in and around the Massachusetts Institute of Technology and thirteen years as Vice-President and Director of Special Projects for the Alfred P. Sloan Foundation.